The Straight Shooter's Guide To Estate Planning

By

Larry V. Parman

Attorney at Law

ISBN 9798815182318

Dedication

I dedicate this book to Mom and Dad – Vance and Avis Parman. Dad, your tragedy inspired me to dedicate my career to helping people protect themselves through proper estate planning. Mom, you were a rock during challenges, mine and your own. To both of you, I could not have asked for better parents. Memories of you lift and inspire me every day.

Praise for
The Straight Shooter's Guide to Estate Planning

"As Oklahoma's former Secretary of State and Secretary of Commerce, Larry Parman has sat at the table with many State Governors and the President of the United States. As a former Dale Carnegie Instructor, he has also taught many ordinary, everyday people - from plumbers, electricians, bankers, business owners, and employees – how to improve their lives. Over the last thirty-five years, few individuals have impressed me more than Larry because he cares so deeply about making a significant impact on others' lives.

In this book, Larry Parman tells it like it is - using his 'in-the-trenches' experience and education to guide you through the estate planning process. The wise say, 'Listen to those who have earned the right to be listened to.' Larry Parman has."

-Mr. and Mrs. Rob Roberts; Edmond, OK

"After a lifetime of working in Estate Planning, I can wholeheartedly endorse Larry Parman's advice. Solid gold for transforming your Legacy!"

-Mark S. Eghrari; Estate Planning Attorney
Smithtown, New York

"We know the value of the estate planning that Larry provides through the ordeal of settling Frank's father's estate. Frank's father did not have an estate plan – only a will. The resulting probate was an expensive experience that took almost two years to complete. That convinced us that we needed to do something different for our estate plan.

We have worked with Larry Parman and his team for over twenty years to care for our estate planning needs. They have done this with careful and diligent attention to the changing laws and rules that government agencies adopt.

We were delighted when we heard Larry had written his third book on estate planning. We know how crucial it is for families to protect themselves, their loved ones, and future generations. This book is like sitting down with Larry for a "fireside chat" as he walks you through setting up your estate plan based on your wishes and needs. As you feel his conviction and passion shine through the pages, we hope you are inspired to transform your legacy from being a burden to your loved ones to creating your own comprehensive, purpose-driven estate plan."

–Mr. and Mrs. Frank Freidhoff; Oklahoma City, OK

"The Straight Shooter's Guide to Estate Planning is written by our attorney, family estate and financial adviser, and long-time friend, Larry V. Parman. Since 1979, Larry has been instrumental in helping our family. He has the knowledge and foresight to guide us and many others through challenging estate, business, tax law changes, residency, career growth, and retirement situations.

You will learn a great deal from the *Straight Shooter's Guide to Estate Planning* and get a taste of what our family has experienced through Larry's guidance for many years. Larry has been a great estate planning counselor. He has assisted us in financial counseling, including the appropriate purchase and structure of life insurance, representing us in buying and selling businesses, and counseling us on various tax issues. He studies and keeps abreast of the law and takes the initiative to make valuable recommendations, which I would categorize as one of the best traits in our relationship.

Larry Parman is also a trusted and valued advisor to our children and grandchildren. We highly endorse him as an excellent estate planner, business attorney, and author.

-Troy L. Wilson, retired Bank Chairman and Chairman of the first Workers' Compensation Commission for the State of Oklahoma, and Elizabeth M. Wilson, retired Bank owner and Director

"As parents, grandparents, and entrepreneurs, we fully understand and appreciate why estate planning is such a critical piece of your life's legacy - both while alive and after you are gone. If you value being responsible for your actions and focusing on what you can control in life, this book is for you. In *Straight Shooter's Guide to Estate Planning*, Larry shows you how to think through and defend against challenges and helps you take advantage of opportunities that you would never have thought about on your own. Larry truly has you and your loved ones' best interests at heart, and he has done everything he can in this book to help you achieve the peace of mind your family deserves."

-Dr. and Mrs. Kelly Brown; Edmond, OK

"The Straight Shooter's Guide To Estate Planning" is not just for "rich" people. It's a book on effective estate planning for anyone: parents, college students, millennials or grandparents. It's for anyone who wants to ensure they have all the I's dotted and T's crossed. It's a book that will assist anyone and everyone with the nuts and bolts of estate planning and lead them to a successful outcome as they apply the straightforward techniques Larry sets forth in this engaging and easy to apply manual.

-Pastor Bill and Barb Schneider

Foreword

In 1993, I co-founded the American Academy of Estate Planning Attorneys (AAEPA), a network of law firms throughout the US, all specializing in estate and elder law planning.

The AAEPA provides its Member firms access to the finest legal research and continuing education available to estate planning firms. Our Member firms are experts in the field.

Larry Parman, and his firm, Parman & Easterday, PLLC, were there at the beginning in 1993 and continue to be valued Members today.Larry and his firm have created estate plans for thousands of families throughout the Midwest. They have become trusted advisors to their clients. Larry was ahead of his time in the mid-1980s when he began offering education events on using a revocable trust as the foundation for an effective estate plan.

His unique approach – offering planning services for a fixed investment, completing the work in 30 days, and guaranteeing client satisfaction set a standard of unparalleled service. Larry's expertise and approach to complex issues have caused multiple generations of families to use his professional services.

I encourage you to read *The Straight Shooter's Guide to Estate Planning* carefully. No one could coach you through the process with more expertise, experience, and thoughtful care for your family than Larry Parman and his team.

Sanford Fisch, President
American Academy of Estate Planning Attorneys

Table of Contents

Preface – My Why

A re you a responsible person?
If the answer is no, feel free to throw this book in the trash bin. If you are, this book provides essential information for you and your family. When you finish reading it, play it forward and share it with someone who might find value in what follows.

After that direct opening, again, if you are still with me and if the answer is, "yes, I am responsible," you will discover how to protect yourself and your family as you experience a condition we know as…life.

Let's get this out of the way right now. No one wakes up in the morning excited about going to an attorney to talk about death and taxes. Yet, we know both are inevitable.

In a letter dated November 13, 1789, which he wrote to the French physicist Jean Baptiste Le Roy, Benjamin Franklin said, "…in this world nothing can be said to be certain, except death and taxes."

As you turn these pages, you will discover what I have learned from helping thousands of families create their estate plans. The words will reveal "best practices" and help you clarify the best steps for you and your family. A pathway will emerge. You will see what works and the challenges awaiting those whose missteps cost their families money and relationships.

My lessons started long ago.

What I discovered on a bookshelf in east Texas triggered my decades-long commitment to helping families avoid the potential catastrophes that can occur when there is no estate plan in place. Here's what happened.

During a summer break from law school, my wife and I visited her parents in east Texas.

The morning started with a round of golf where my father-in-law, Harold Trammell, schooled me on the importance of keeping the ball in the fairway. His excellent short game inside of 100 yards and a reliable putting stroke trumped my ability to outdrive him. That day was no different. I handed him another $5 at a time when I did not have $5 to lose.

We drove back to his house to watch a football game following the round. Harold kept admiring my $5 bill in his hand. It was not the first time I had increased his net worth on the golf course.

Hello Norman Dacey

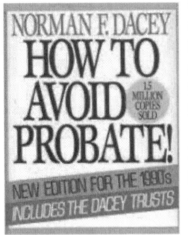

One of the teams called a time-out. I stood up and walked over to the bookshelf next to the television. I was curious about the books that were of interest to Darlene's parents. I was hoping to find a book titled, *How to Beat Your Father-in-Law in Golf.* No luck. However, one book title caught my eye. I pulled down their copy of *How to Avoid Probate* by Norman Dacey.

After opening it, the game became meaningless. After a few pages, Mr. Dacey had my full attention. There was no class in law school teaching us about helping families avoid the costly and time-consuming probate process that follows the death of a family member.

How to Avoid Probate took dead aim at the probate system and lawyers who perpetuated it. It advocated the use of trusts to avoid the probate process's costs, delay, and publicity. The book described how to set up estates by including sample trust forms and instructions for readers to use.

Mr. Dacey's book criticized the unnecessarily high fees deducted from estates during the probate process. He unmasked the soft underbelly of probate. The book infuriated the lawyers. He was going after the bread-and-butter part of some law practices. Dacey thought probate was a scam. It did set well with lawyers because Dacey was not a lawyer.

What happened next?

The American Bar Association was quite critical of the book. Publication of the book led to many lawsuits. In one instance, the New York County Lawyers Association sued him for the unauthorized practice of law.

Mr. Dacey eventually won in 1967 when the New York Court of Appeals stopped the efforts of New York lawyers to ban Dacey's book. The Court held publication and distribution of self-help law materials with forms and instructions to complete the forms was constitutionally protected free speech under the First Amendment and not the unauthorized practice of law.

That did not stem the lawsuits that followed in other states.

Meanwhile, the book sold over two million copies. That alone should tell you about the importance of this "controversial" book.

Dacey continued his effort to educate people on how to avoid probate, keep their assets out of court and transfer those assets quickly and efficiently to their heirs. Norman F. Dacey made one thing clear. He was a hostile force against attorneys and the probate court and was not going away. He paved the way for trusts to be the most commonly used method to transfer wealth from one generation to the next at minimum cost, effort, and in the most practical manner.

More than anyone, Dacey changed the paradigm of what was possible for most people when creating their estate plans. Before Dacey, most people viewed probate as something that "just had to happen" following one's death. A default future, if you will.

Dacey transformed that notion. Before distributing our estates, we were no longer bound to that default future of probate, court proceedings, and time delays. What was now possible was a created future, giving us greater control and making the transfer of assets to our heirs much easier.

As transformational as Dacey's book was, even he failed to account for the tremendous lifecare planning opportunities afforded by a revocable trust. We will explore that benefit in some detail.

As I mentioned, Dacey's message was compelling. Upon returning home, I ordered a copy and continued to study the material. There was no discussion about avoiding probate in law school. I filed that away in the back of my mind.

Then, the unexpected occurred. Before going to the unexpected, hold on to Norman Dacey's advice as I describe the next critical experience for me and how it impacted my career.

The Unexpected

On the way home from the office, I stopped by a hospital to visit a family friend recovering from a two-year battle with cancer. The physical, mental, and emotional challenges had taken their toll. Charlie and his wife Mildred lost their only child, his wife, and their only two grandchildren two years earlier in a private plane crash. That compounded the challenges of cancer.

After a nearly two-hour visit with Charlie, I headed home. After walking into the house, my wife, Darlene, was eager to hear about Charlie. I told her I felt great about our conversation. "Charlie decided to live today. He is thinking about the future, not just about his illness, not just about his depression, not just about the tragedy of the past. He spoke about the future, his future, and his future with Mildred. I could not have been happier.

Then it happened.

Ten minutes later, at about 9 P.M., the phone rang. I answered and heard the voice of a family friend from my hometown. While in the military, I learned about a strategy intended to weaken and disrupt the enemy. You attack from the air before a ground invasion. Soften the beaches, they say. "Larry, your dad was in an accident this morning at the farm. It doesn't look good. I'll keep you posted." My mind raced.

"Larry, He's Gone"

That call softened the beaches of my expectations and left me bewildered. Fifteen minutes later came the worst. "Larry, he's gone." What? What do you mean, "He's gone?" How can that be? I talked to him yesterday afternoon. Dad was 56 and in excellent physical and mental condition. My parents were beginning to experience the financial benefit from decades of hard work and sacrifice. "Gone? What in the world are you talking about?"

For the previous two days, Vance Parman had a sore throat. He quickly stopped to visit the doctor, who recommended he not work that day, not be around people for a couple of days, and go light on conversation. Dad followed the doctor's orders, left Mom a note, and went to the farm. He jumped on the John Deere 4020 and headed toward a field full of large, round hay bales. They needed to be gathered up and organized in rows closer to the barn.

On the side of a hill, he backed the tractor toward a bale. He embedded the forks into the bale, elevated it off the ground with a hydraulic lift, shifted gears, moved forward, and made a hard-right turn to avoid the nearby deep ditch.

Then, the centrifugal force of the 1,000-pound (plus) bale and the damp grass caused the tractor to start sliding sideways toward the ditch. The two left wheels slipped off the edge. That set the tractor's destiny. It rolled over him as it headed toward the bottom of the ditch. The tractor ended up on all fours and started rolling backward. It pinned Dad's left leg under the left rear tire. He could not undo the damage he incurred in the fall and could not get out from underneath the tire.

Suddenly, I understood my friend's meaning when he said, "...Larry, he's gone."

Many of you have lost your parents. How did losing my father relate to this book?

It impacted my life in every possible, imaginable way.

The Disappointment

My dad died without an estate plan in place. We had discussed it, but he had too many other items on his 'To Do' list, like some of you reading this. There were just too many "important" matters to attend to every day. How could creating an estate plan be that important?

At that point in my career, I was in the investment business. With my law degree and bar membership in hand, I strongly encouraged mom and dad to create a plan. It did not happen. Here's the disappointing part. He knew they needed to get something put in place. He put it off and ran out of time.

Let me ask you: if you knew there was no tomorrow in your future, would estate planning be important?

A couple of years before finishing this book, I lost my mother, Avis. What a jewel. She never remarried. We were in their home in Northwest Missouri, going through everything in the house. I volunteered to sift through 75 years of their lives together and then mom's in the years following dad's death. Mom saved every card she ever received. I moved through the boxes, file by file.

I opened one of Dad's file folders and instantly recognized his signature on the letters he had written. Then, I came across a tattered and worn 3x5 card in his handwriting. Dad was a list maker. He favored 3x5 cards to prioritize what he would accomplish on any day, week, month, or year. Dad wrote this particular card the year before his death. I read it slowly, then stopped, my eyes transfixed on one line. There it was. Notice one of the items at the end of part II? It reads:

Other: Establish Trust

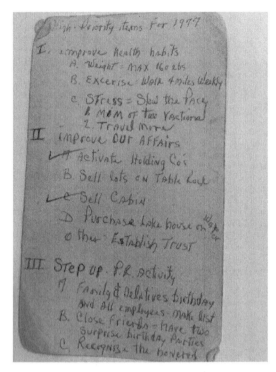

There is no check mark indicating completion. There is no line drawn through the goal indicating completion. No estate plan at all.

What were the consequences? Our family endured over two years of probating the estate and three years arguing with the I.R.S. about the value of farmland and a small, closely-held business.

Nightmare.

Consciousness and alertness activate by the combined workings of the brain stem. The brain stem consists of the cerebrum and the spinal cord. Together, they form the reticular activating system located deep within the upper part of the brain stem. Going through this process with my mother triggered the memories and lessons from Norman Dacey's book, *How to Avoid Probate.* It put me on high alert.

That experience changed my life. My dad – my best friend – was gone. Now informed by my personal experience and the lessons from Norman Dacey's book, at some point in the probate and I.R.S. dance, I realized that my experience must be shared with others. I knew that if I ever set up my law practice, I would spend every waking moment standing in front of groups, visiting with families one-on-one, sharing the importance of creating an estate plan.

The Accidental Inspiration

In 1985, I founded the Parman & Easterday law firm. Today, I continue sharing that message with as much passion as possible. Inadvertently, and unfortunately, my dad, Vance Parman, became the inspirational founder of our firm.

The experience with my family remains the "Why" I chose to be an estate planning attorney. It led to our firm's Purpose.

Our firm is committed to ensuring our family of clients has a life of abundance, healthy relationships, and the peace of mind from knowing they have done the right thing to protect themselves and their families.

We create a partnership with our families to discover what's truly important to them and collaborate to design a plan that gives them the peace of mind that occurs when they know they have taken action to protect themselves, their families, and their assets.

Because of the experience with my father's estate, I understand the pain that families endure when there is an estate planning failure. I want to help them avoid that.

Most of our law firm's team members have endured their personal experiences with the consequences of inadequate estate planning.

A loved one, call him Sam, was adamant about not going into a nursing home in one case. "I will never go into a nursing home." Yet he was admitted after he fell and could not be lifted to his feet. Because they were unprepared, the cost assaulted their financial condition.

More troubling than the economic damage was the damage to relationships. Despite Sam's wife's longtime plea to do some planning, he resisted. "Why do we need to do that...spend that money...when I'm dead, it won't matter...the kids can figure it out.'

Can you guess the residual bitterness? The price of self-centeredness and the lack of caring about his family was all too evident.

In another instance with Joe. Joe became disabled with no plan in place. No one was authorized to act on his behalf. He thought having a 20-year-old last will was sufficient. He did not realize a last will does nothing for you during your lifetime because it does not go into effect until death.

That's the risk of misinformation and disinformation.

We have structured our firm and our processes in order to help people avoid the calamities of Vance, Sam, and Joe.

Failing to plan creates expenses and time delays that can decimate an estate overnight. Our work helps people minimize costs and time delays and protect their assets, regardless of what might occur during their lifetime.

Mainly, we want the people working with us to sense our focus on them to understand their concerns. We want to listen so we have clarity about their goals carefully. We want to partner with them to develop a plan. We seek ways that allow our expertise to shine. We offer a sense of empathy they might not experience with other attorneys.

That is what we aspire to in working with our clients. We remember the rule: "We have two ears and one mouth." We think that is the appropriate proportion between listening and speaking. When we have a conversation with clients about their situation, goals, concerns, and objectives, we must be good listeners.

Our approach centers on more than just knowing the law or being experts. I mean, knowing the law is the minimum hurdle, right?

The key is our experience. It gives us the ability to   ask the appropriate, targeted, directed, and meaningful questions that will help people get in touch with their ideas and feelings about what they want to have happen at specific points in their lives.

And like I said, I use the term "partner" because we like to feel like we work with our family of clients as partners. Whether we help them create an estate plan, help them sell a business, or save assets from nursing home expenses, we act as their partners. Providing those services does not represent a transaction for us. Our process is goal-oriented and nurturing. It is an experience that continues and deepens our relationship until the end.

When people work with us, it might be uncomfortable to think about these things, but it's an essential nurturing experience that we share with them.

While every estate planning client has their unique DNA, most of the challenges they have are personal and occur within their family.

To no one's surprise, those challenges can impede people's opening up and sharing essential facts to achieve their goals. There may be issues occurring – or have occurred - in their family that cause discomfort, and they may not want to talk about them.

Our objective, occasionally a challenge, is to let people know they are not alone. All families have issues. All families have matters that might be a little uncomfortable to discuss. We try to make it clear to them and share the importance of taking steps to address those issues and not shy away from them. It reduces the likelihood that circumstances and events overcome or overwhelm the family when they are gone. Some families are well prepared for this; others are not.

> **Be a person who acts with intention and is not someone governed by circumstances.**

Sometimes mom and dad have been the glue that kept everything together. When they are gone, everything falls apart.

Other families and other parents move toward their issues. While things may not be perfect within their family, most of our clients work to enable conversations with their families about the plan they are creating and share their expectations. They get clear with everyone that they have made their intentions clear and that family members are to be respectful to their siblings and advisors when they are gone.

We make every effort to create the perfect estate plan for our clients at that time in their lives. Yet, I remind them that regardless of how carefully you create a plan, damaged relationships between and among family members and siblings can throw the process off course. Family dysfunction rears its ugly head in the most surprising places, at the most inopportune time.

It can be triggered by arguing about who gets to keep the original copy of the family photo album, or a personal keepsake, or the house, or who is named as the successor trustee or personal representative of the estate and has responsibility for wrapping up the estate and making appropriate distributions. These factors should be discussed and considered in the planning process.

Bad behavior can ruin a good plan.

There is wisdom in educating our families about your plan and your expectations. Having intentional conversations with your family will help things go smoother down the road.

Now here we are, still addressing a public health crisis. We should not have to depend on a pandemic to cause us to take action and do the right thing for our families. We should do it because of the love relationship with our families. We should do it because it's the smart thing to do, the right thing to do. Regardless, Covid-19 has cast its light on our country and created a new reality:

Estate planning is no longer optional. It's mandatory!

It is mandatory, not just for your family. It is mandatory for you for maximum protection during your lifetime and at your passing. Most people fail to think about issues they will face during their lifetime – illness, disability, a long-term nursing home stay, even incapacity. So, who should be concerned about creating an estate plan? The following answer might surprise you.

Here's the first no-holds-barred, Straight-Shooter's point. The reasons families create an estate plan are nearly infinite. The real reason to get your estate plan in place is that you know it is the right thing - the smart thing - to do for your family. If you do not believe that, read no further. If you cannot start with accepting that theorem, you will reject all the material that follows. Fret not. Netflix has a new series about to start.

If you are still with me, great. We are going to add to your existing knowledge base. We are going to address the critical factors to consider, including how to approach estate planning strategies and create an Action Plan that will allow you to have the peace of mind you may be seeking but may have, thus far, failed to achieve.

Stay with me, hold your biases at bay, and *The Straight Shooter's Guide to Estate Planning* will open new possibilities for you and your family. We are also registered investment advisors, and these new possibilities will sprinkle a few straight-shooter points about your investment decisions. We will share a few ideas about how you can avoid the mistakes that cost investors millions and shatter people's American Dream, especially during their precious retirement years.

I invite you to read and fully digest the *Straight Shooter's Guide*. In this era of information overload, fact-checking, misinformation, fiction, and "expert opinion" presented as fact, it is high time for straight-shooting talk about this critical topic.

Let us start here. Estate planning is part art and part science. The process is not entirely formulaic, nor is it a one-size-fits-all area of the law.

Of course, specific estate planning strategies must be part of the planning process. Statutes, regulations, I.R.S Revenue and Letter Rulings, and case law influence those strategies. Those represent the science component of estate planning. How that science relates to you in designing your family strategy depends on your unique situation. That is the art.

What we have covered in this chapter leads to a critical question. Who should read this book?

Who Should Read This Book?

E veryone.

Years of experience lead me to conclude that estate planning is all about "asset protection." And everyone reading this book has assets worth protecting from the known and the unknown threats we encounter daily.

Every person who has attained the age of majority and every family needs an estate plan that protects themselves and their assets. Each person should have an estate plan that addresses their unique asset protection needs.

For some families, asset protection is satisfied by avoiding probate. For others, it extends to eliminating or minimizing taxes. For others, it extends even further to protecting family assets from nursing home expenses that can decimate an estate. It may include a desire to successfully sell a business or farm and ranch operation or transition ownership of those businesses to the next generation.

Asset protection may extend beyond that to include divorce and remarriage issues, avoiding predators and creditors, protecting a spendthrift child from themselves, or ensuring an inheritance is protected for a child with special needs.

I could reverse the question posed by the chapter heading and ask, "who wouldn't want to know how to take care of their estate and outline what they want to occur if something happens to them?"

Now we address why everyone should read the book.

The New Context for Estate Planning

We must talk about the world in which we live. Demographics, life expectancy, litigation, bankruptcies, divorces, shoddy legal work, mixed marriages and families, people "sandwiched" in between caregiving for aging parents and young adults, exploding nursing home expenses, and other factors are now present in the estate planning equation.

Society is changing – rapidly. The evolution in demographic makeup and psychographic preferences is profound. Population growth alone is stunning. In 1969 there were 207 million people in the United States. As of this writing, there are nearly 335 million and counting. The composition of the family unit is changing – rapidly. The number of cohabitating singles is changing – rapidly. The population is aging rapidly. These, and other factors, play an essential role in creating an estate plan.

In the early days of my practice, most of our clients fit a predictable profile. They mainly were in long-term marriages. There were two or more children. Many lived in the same house for most of their marriage. Some were retired or nearing retirement. Others might have been a long-time employees with a pension. There were current or former business owners. We helped those who had significant farm and ranch operations. Some clients were financially independent. Most were not wealthy but were prudent with their money and had accumulated a nest egg that would see them through their retirement years in comfort.

Things have changed. People today are more willing to remarry, even into their 80s and 90s. That willingness, and the high divorce rates in the U.S., contribute to the number of our citizens now in their second or third marital relationship. Demographic changes are occurring at a rapid rate. People are more mobile and are moving to other states, either to pursue new opportunities or for retirement. Through their policies, states and cities compete for companies and individuals to relocate and people are responding.

Longevity also impacts estate and financial planning. For the highest income earners, life expectancy at age 50 is 91.1 years for females, 88.8 years for males.[1] This means trustees (the person or entity with the fiduciary responsibility to manage and oversee trust assets) will manage trust assets based on the assumption of longer life spans for current beneficiaries. Children will be much older when they inherit, and they may inherit less.

What constitutes a "household" has changed dramatically over the past decades. In the 1950's, married couples comprised nearly 80% of households in the U.S. Today, it is less than 50%. According to one study, the fastest-growing segment of our population is unmarried

---

[1] "The Growing Gap in Life Expectancy by Income: Implications for Federal Programs and Responses", The National Academies of Sciences, Engineering, and Medicine, Washington, D.C., National Academies Press (September 17, 2015).

heterosexual couples.[2] Another mentions that in 1960, nearly 60% of adults ages 18-29 were married; today, only 18% of that age cohort is married.[3] It is not just young people who are staying single. According to research by Anthony Cilluffo and D'Vera Cohn, the number of older adults cohabitating has increased 75% in the last ten years.[4] Planning with a non-citizen spouse presents different challenges as well.

With one of the highest divorce rates globally, divorces in the U.S. are becoming more common among Boomers, often resulting in remarriage and a blending of families or cohabitation at some point. Forty-two million adults in the U.S. have been married more than once. Nearly one-sixth of American children grow up in blended families, and 40% of us have at least one step relative.[5]

Then, you have the issue of the three-parent family, where a second spouse has parental rights over the children of the first marriage. Nearly one-third of families deal with the challenge of having no children. Roughly the same percentage are traditional families comprised of heterosexual, married couples with children. Almost the same percentage rate are modern families consisting of either blended, same-sex, or single parents.

These changes add complexity to the estate planning process not present when I started my practice. There are more challenges.

---

[2] "The Growing Gap in Life Expectancy by Income: Implications for Federal Programs and Responses", The National Academies of Sciences, Engineering, and Medicine, Washington, D.C., National Academies Press (September 17, 2015).
[3] Paul Taylor and the Pew Research Center, *The Next America: Boomers, Millennials and The Looming Generational Showdown* (Public Affairs 2016).]
[4] Anthony Cilluffo and D'Vera Cohn, "10 Demographic Trends Shaping the U.S. and the World in 2017, Pew Research Center (April, 27, 2017.
[5] *Obergefell v. Hodges*, 135 S. Ct. 2584, 2623 (2015).

> ## Shifting demographics make the need for planning more important.

Recent estimates say over 40 million lawsuits were filed in the U.S. by one of the approximately 1.3 million registered attorneys. We have 3,769 lawyers per one million people in the U.S, compared to Japan with 287 attorneys per one million people. No, you did not misread that. Differences in the two judicial systems are among the reasons cited for the difference. Yet, we know we have a very litigious legal system in the United States.

No one likes to talk about the large number of lawsuits filed each year due to poorly designed and implemented Wills and trusts. Trusts are difficult to challenge, yet probate courts are a forum for disgruntled family members challenging provisions of last Wills. When you challenge a Will, you question the validity of the Will itself. Some decide to challenge a Will because they believe undue influence, fraud, forgery, or lack of mental capacity (testamentary capacity) played a role. Here's an example.

When we created Sally's estate plan, she arranged for her assets to be shared equally between her children. The daughter, Susie, lived with Sally during her declining years. After Sally's passing and contrary to her long-stated wishes, we discover she executed a Will giving 100% of her estate to Susie. What triggered the change? Was it because Susie provided care for her during the last years of her life? Who drove the decision? Did Sally possess the mental capacity required to execute a document that made such a profound change? Susie's brother Jim might contest the Will because Susie exercised undue influence over her mother during that period. What was Sally's intent? Were other factors involved? What role did Susie play in the apparent change of heart? The opportunities for litigation are endless. But that's not all.

On average, over 750,000 bankruptcies are filed in the U.S. every year. As many as 25% of them are because of overwhelming medical bills.

Nearly 50 million of our citizens are caregivers, often "sandwiched" in between aging parents needing help and young adult children who may still be living at home and are at least somewhat dependent on their parents.

Nursing Homes and other long-term care expenses are out of control. Did you know the average cost of a Nursing Home in America now exceeds $100,000 per year? I just went through that with my mother in a town of 900 people. The nursing home cost was nearly $7,000 per month.

And we cannot forget the genuine dangers of the Coronavirus and other global health issues confronting us today. Or the economic impact of what our country has felt since March 2020. The suffering extends well past the tragic loss of lives due to the virus into the living death created by economic failure, depression, and other disorders now coming to our attention. The social and political upheaval and violence we recently witnessed in the streets of our country compounds the problem.

A summary of this context means estate planning has more variables than when I began my practice. According to a study by the University of Michigan, divorced adults have the highest rates of intestacy (dying without a will) in the U.S. The University of Michigan study revealed that while the overall intestacy rate among those 50 and older is 42%, the rate rises to 62% among divorced adults. Having no plan is a recipe for disaster, especially in blended families.

Along with these medical, cultural, demographic, and political shifts, the law is also changing. For example, typically, state law forbids a trust to last in perpetuity. The *Rule Against Perpetuities* states that the longest a trust can last is "lives in being plus 21 years". Translated, that means that when you die, your youngest grandchild is, say, 10, any trust you create can last until the grandchild dies plus 21 years. Given life expectancies today, that approximates 100 -110 years. However, at least 23 states have either repealed this rule or vastly lengthened the mandatory vesting or termination date for trusts. In those states, there is no limit on how long a trust can exist for the benefit of your heirs and descendants.

Shifting marital choices create a new context for planning.

A few weeks ago, I learned that a long-time client is getting remarried. He is 87. The number of people getting remarried between 70 and 90 is growing. According to the Pew Research Center, in 2017, over 50% of adults over 65 will remarry at some point in their life. In 1960, only 55% of people 55-64 who left a previous marriage went on to remarry. By comparison, in 2013, that number was 67%. Multiple marriages may work great for the two new spouses.

In some cases, the children of both families are supportive. In other remarriages, that is not the case. It is a fertile ground for animosity and contention.

A side note. We have had this experience. Two separate couples retain us to help them create an estate plan. In both instances, a spouse passes away. A little later, the surviving spouses marry. They were surprised and delighted to find out our firm created the estate plan for both original couples.

It is clear. These changing dynamics create multiple challenges in the context of estate planning. The opportunities for confusion and mischief increase, sometimes dramatically. The potential discord and chaos leads to one conclusion.

Everyone needs to read this book.

Who Should Have an Estate Plan?

S ame answer. Everyone.

If you are single, by choice, or because you are divorced or have lost a spouse, you need a plan.

If you have experienced multiple marriages, you need a plan. This is especially true if you and your new spouse have separate children, or perhaps children by prior marriage and children together. The latter situation presents significant planning challenges.

If you are a young adult over 18, you need a plan. You are now legally responsible for your behaviors, actions, and decision-making. Your plan may not deal with a significant number of assets. Yet, you need a plan that empowers someone to act on your behalf for financial transactions and make medical decisions for you if you can no longer make them yourself.

Parents may be thinking, "Surely, I can make medical decisions for my 19-year-old college student if they run into trouble." Well, maybe you can. Perhaps you can't make that decision on behalf of that young adult child. Why assume the risk? The fact you have never thought about this does not make it untrue.

Young adults need an advance directive, sometimes referred to as a living will. They need a healthcare power of attorney. They need a HIPAA form: a Privacy Act document they sign that grants the medical community permission to share information about their medical situation with family members and others they may select. They need those documents to cover routine medical emergencies and health care matters if something happens to them.

For example, sometimes people say, "I'm too young." Hold that thought. If you have minor children, single or married, go out to a party one night, and do not come home, what happens?

How will your mortgage be handled? Will your children be required to leave their childhood home? What happens if you're married and both of you are killed in an accident? Who will be the guardians of your minor children? Will there be a fight between and among family members over who should be the guardian? If so, these disputes usually end up in court.

Again, failing to plan means you have added to the headaches and heartaches of those you leave behind.

Then we have the Sandwich Generation, those of you caring for aging parents and supporting young adults, many of whom are still dependents, living at home, and on the other hand, you are caring for aging parents. They may be living with you. They may be living independently but need assistance or may be in a nursing home. You may have family members facing deteriorating health and may be coming face to face with the reality of entering a nursing home. If any of those situations are familiar, this book will be helpful.

If you are a retiree, you need a plan that addresses life planning, asset protection, retirement account distributions, and beneficiary designations. You need a plan addressing who will manage and receive your estate, and oversee investment performance, cash flow, and long-term health care (assisted living and nursing home) costs, among other issues.

If you are within a few years of retirement, you need a plan. Your planning will be somewhat more anticipatory. To ensure you will be financially protected once retirement occurs, you will undoubtedly address the issues identified in the previous paragraph and consider how to improve your current estate plan, investment plan, and tax plan.

You need a plan if you are a business owner or farm and ranch owner. Your issues will include those previously mentioned, plus others of equal importance. For example, what is your business succession plan? How is it to be implemented? How do you implement it fairly for children who may not be involved in running the business? What are the financial terms? Does a sale to a third party or insiders make more sense? There are dozens of questions and issues to address for business owners and farm and ranch operators.

Everyone Has Their Own Unique Estate Planning DNA

Estate planning DNA is a web of entanglements, including the family's current situation with strands of goals, challenges, financial concerns, capabilities, interests, priorities, and commitments, all tightly woven in and around the family unit. Every family we have worked with has its own unique set of circumstances and estate planning DNA. That means each plan we create is different in some regard.

Another critical point is that each person's life experience creates a unique worldview. Included in that view is an opinion about whether estate planning is important enough to act.

Be clear: either create your plan of what happens to you during your life, your disability, and your death, or someone else will create it for you. My goal is to inspire you to overcome estate planning lethargy and give you the confidence to move forward. You will either learn a few new things from this book or perhaps fill in a few missing points that are important to your decision.

We know knowledge alone is not enough. Knowledge without action is almost worthless. What you experience from this book may not rise to the level of an epiphany. However, it will let you discover new possibilities and see a pathway to complete your plan successfully.

Everyone needs a plan. Yet, we hear people repeat various concerns about planning, often elevating those concerns to objections. Objections become excuses. Excuses morph into rationalizing that nothing needs to be done. Once that mindset takes root, people fail to act in their self-interest, fail to protect themselves, and fail to protect their families by planning.

Why? Let's take a closer look at why people resist estate planning.

Blind Spots, The Occurring, and Biases

This chapter is for those of us procrastinating, who just cannot seem to pull the trigger on getting a great estate plan. Stay with it. What follows is important. Recognizing these principles has been influential in my life. They can be for yours. The principles will help in many areas of your life, not just estate planning.

People often fail to plan because they do not recognize their blind spots. Blind spots, how things occur to us, and biases can lead to misguided thinking. Misguided thinking leads to poor decision-making

Something may occur to us as "difficult." Blind spots contain solutions and issues we do not even know exist. Our biases override rational thought. All lead to procrastination. Procrastination leads to an absence of action. Failure to act in the estate planning arena too often leads to disaster. It guarantees you have increased the odds that you and your family will become estate planning victims. That's what happened with my parents.

Blind Spots

Everyone has blind spots. They are present in our professional life and our personal life. They impact our relationships and outcomes in our lives. Failure to recognize the presence of blind spots can lead to bad decisions and sometimes disastrous results.

Think of a circle. Inside that circle is All the Knowledge in the World. Now imagine that circle divided up into three sections. What We Know would be the smallest section compared to All the Knowledge in the World. The What We Know section reflects what you already know – how to speak, comb your hair, drive a car, look up a word in the dictionary, perform the tasks required of your employment, tie your shoes, and the names of your family members, and so forth.

Another section of the circle is larger. It represents What We Know We Don't Know. For me, that would be things like carrying on a conversation in Swahili with a group of Maasai children in Tanzania (their English was excellent), flying a 787 Dreamliner, or performing micro-surgery to remove a tumor from the inside of someone's bladder.

These two sections – What We Know and What We Know We Don't Know – are similar in that they are both in the realm of what we know. I know how to drive my car. I know I do not know Swahili. Educating ourselves makes it possible to move items from the What We Don't Know section of the circle to the What We Know section of the circle.

The third section of the circle is by far the largest. Within the All the Knowledge in the World circle, this section contains all the Things

We Don't Know We Don't Know. This section takes up far more than most of the space within the circle.

What does this mean in the context of estate planning? We struggle to understand what could or should be done. We hesitate to formulate a plan of action because we are blind to the fact that we don't even know what we don't know.

I know much about estate planning, but would you trust me to perform brain surgery on you or a loved one? For me to understand that and fail to acknowledge it creates a blind spot. If I acted on that and someone allowed me to perform brain surgery on them, the outcome would not be good.

There are blind spots in our lives. They shut us down. We often fail to recognize the phenomena and their impact on our lives. Blind spots remain hidden in the circle section called We Don't Know What We Don't Know. Acknowledging the presence of blind spots helps draw them into the open and can alter our perceptions about estate planning and our life.

"Unknown to you" can also create havoc. When we make a decision based on a belief that we know something when we don't, the outcome may not be what we wanted. Most of us hate to admit that. We love telling people, "My research showed me that...." But what if that research is filtered through a "not knowing"? More on that in a moment.

Not that many years ago, when we realized it was time to create an estate plan and were unsure about how to proceed, we would reach out to others for guidance. We sought third-party opinions. We made inquiries of friends, family, CPAs, investment advisors, or insurance agents. We assumed these people either had the expertise to set us on the right path or would at least be honest with us.

Today, the evaluation process has changed. The inquiries continue. However, now we often start with an online search to discover the holy grail of estate and financial planning. We hope the answer pops out and hits us like a Joe Frazier left hook (he's a former heavy-weight boxing champion known for this devasting left hook punch). We are trying to move the What We Don't Know over to the What We Know section of the circle. Instead, in many cases, we discover so much misinformation and disinformation from our online searches that we end up being more uncertain than we were before we began the journey.

We circle back to friends, family, and advisors. We might go to ten different lawyers and ask them the same question. We get 12 different answers. Everyone has a different opinion. Some have experienced the perils of poor planning. That discourages us even more. Then we realize something else is occurring.

The Occurring

When we begin thinking about estate planning, we start hearing the chatter inside our brains. It's as if a little person with a loud voice is sitting on our shoulder, constantly yapping away. With the constant barrage, the occurring to us becomes:

- Why am I even doing this? I don't have enough money to worry about or even plan. Why would I waste my time and money doing it?
- I don't know what to do.

- There are too many hard decisions to make. I have to decide who will manage my estate when I'm gone.
- If I become incapacitated, who is going to take care of me?
- Is this going to cost a lot of money? NOTE: Compared to what? Doing nothing?
- I don't know who to trust to help me.

The misinformation and disinformation and the constant chatter we hear from the little person on our shoulders create doubt and a lack of comfort. We lose our confidence. We become confused. We shut down. We do nothing.

Our actions correlate with how the world is occurring to us. At this point, the estate planning world is occurring to us as, "This is just too hard, too confusing, too overwhelming."

There is another pathway, one that creates a new possibility, one that will help you sort through the confusion. Principles contained in the book *The Three Laws of Performance* allow us to examine what contributes to us doing nothing and leaving ourselves and our family vulnerable.

> **How people perform (act or not act) correlates to how a situation occurs to them.**

The *First Law of Performance* states that how people perform (act or not act) correlates to how a situation occurs to them. If estate planning is occurring to us as "...too hard, confusing, don't know who to trust, it's overwhelming...." that locks us down.

How a situation occurs to us arises in language.

The *Second Law of Performance* states that how a situation occurs to us arises in language. Again, if the language we are hearing ourselves say, or hearing from that little guy on our shoulder, or hearing from others, is "…too hard, confusing, do not know who to trust, overwhelming…" it should be no surprise that once again, we lock down. Doubt and fear appear. We live into a default future of "doing nothing" because we continue to use the same descriptive language we have used in the past.

When this becomes our way of thinking, we are then standing for doing nothing. Be assured that doing nothing will make our family and us victims of the estate planning process. If we decide to do nothing, our family pays the price. People get caught up in the language they listen to, do not follow through, and leave too many loose ends.

When we continue using that language to govern our actions into the future, a default future of the same Do-Nothing outcome occurs unless we break the pattern.

Future-based language transforms how situations occur to people.

The *Third Law of Performance* shows the way to a new possibility. It states that future-based language transforms how situations occur to us. Let's leave the descriptive language behind and tell that guy on our shoulder to quiet down. Instead, we can work from a clean whiteboard and utilize language to transform our estate planning attitude and take action to protect ourselves and our families.

Instead of declarative statements, half of which are untrue, why not reframe the statements into discovery questions? That helps sift through all the clutter and gives us the confidence we need to proceed with our plan.

Start here. Virtually everyone says they do not want to be a burden to their children. Is that true for you? If so, declare it. Repeatedly. Write it down. Identify possible ways you might become a burden to your children. Use the language of possibility. Declare there is a pathway for you to protect yourself and your family. Declare there are professionals to help me. Declare this is an investment, not a cost. Declare there will be peace of mind upon completing this critical step in your life.

Leaving an estate planning mess does not reduce the burden you may create. Write down exactly what you prepared to do. By when?

Congratulations! You have begun the journey from paralysis to action to accomplishment.

Biases

Some researchers say over 100 biases influence our thinking, therefore, our actions. Two forms of bias deserve mention – confirmation bias and cognitive dissonance.

Confirmation bias is our tendency to see all evidence as supporting our existing beliefs, even if the evidence is nothing more than a coincidence. We may extensively research a topic and completely ignore evidence contrary to what we believed before the research.

Cognitive dissonance occurs when we rationalize why our actions are inconsistent with our beliefs. We believe one thing and do another. We believe in being physically fit yet overeat. Human beings are rationalizing machines. For example, we believe we don't want to be a burden to our children, yet we refuse to take action to keep that from happening. Remember my question in the Preface? Are you a responsible person? We may believe we are, but we fail to confirm it by acting responsibly regarding our estate planning. How can we think we're responsible yet do nothing to protect ourselves and our family?

> **Confirmation bias and cognitive dissonance
> can lead to poor decision-making.**

The challenge is not the amount of information that is available. The bigger problem is there is almost too much information. There is so much misinformation and disinformation about estate planning that it seems overwhelming.

One point bears repeating. Remember when I said that everyone has unique estate planning DNA? We become confused when we become overwhelmed with the volume of information and the conflicting number of possible solutions. Then we start listening to the wrong people. We may consult friends, relatives, neighbors, and even professionals who, while well-intended, may have no clue or expertise.

Concerns Can Become Excuses

We now know we take actions in our life based on how the world, or a situation, is occurring to us. That is also true for the estate planning process. Most concerns we hear expressed about estate planning directly reflect how the world is occurring to that person about the estate planning process. How the world is occurring to them about estate planning directly impacts what actions they're willing to take. Perhaps most importantly, when they are willing to take them.

If what is occurring sounds like: It's expensive; it's hard; I don't like attorneys; my sister created a plan, and it didn't work; I don't want to make that decision; I can't decide; I don't know; or, most sinister – I don't care; let them figure it out; it's their problem, you are not going to do anything.

Deciding to get your financial and estate house in order is a love decision. "I don't care" is a declaration about how estate planning is occurring to you and how you feel about your family. You may be a victim of confirmation bias. Or cognitive dissonance.

It might sound like this if we apply the concepts of blind spots, occurring, and biases to actual conversations with clients.

People express concern about the exploding costs of long-term health care and how that might impact the legacy they leave their children. The unfortunate truth is that some of us – more than we believe – will end up in a nursing home or experience in-home long-term health care.

People are concerned about government interference and privacy. They want to ensure that what decisions they make about their estate plans stay within the family unit and their chosen professional advisors.

They want to be sure that their assets are transferred to their heirs as quickly and efficiently. They do not want the government getting in the way. Nor do they want lawyers, bureaucrats, or the court system to delay the process.

Of course, everyone wants to minimize tax. The worst thing that can happen is that you fail to plan and pay more in tax than the law requires you to pay. This past week I met with a gentleman who was referred to us. He previously paid me a retainer to review his current plan. We were in our second meeting. He has a $12 million estate, virtually all assets are owned in his name, his wife has Alzheimer's, and his only daughter has early-onset dementia and is deteriorating fast. He has supported his daughter's family for years. He has a horrible relationship with his son-in-law. A few years ago, he spent a considerable amount of money with an attorney who set up an excellent plan but failed to work with his client to implement the plan properly. The money spent on setting up the plan was wasted.

With no additional planning and assuming values remain the same, after January 1, 2026, upon this gentleman's death this family will owe approximately $2 million in estate tax. They will pay estate tax they are not legally obligated to pay! Think about the issues that will confront this family if he dies first. He came up with so many excuses not to move forward. I returned the unused retainer and told him I would not let him waste more money on planning unless he was willing to follow through and take the steps needed to implement the plan.

Think about how blind spots, biases, and how planning was occurring to him. Of course, it is his decision. It is an expensive decision; nonetheless, it remains his.

Yes, that horrible outcome is possible. That example disproves the notion that everyone wants to minimize taxes and protect their family.

There is another significant concern expressed more frequently than in past years. It did not occur in the earlier stages of my practice. I mentioned it earlier. Suppose one spouse dies, then the surviving spouse remarries a few years later. What is the impact?

When I visit with married clients about this issue, the conversation teeters between humor, denial, and quiet reflection. Thorough planning requires we address the issue. What protection do you want in place in the event a remarriage occurs?

Sometimes, to deflect the seriousness of the question, I have heard one of the spouses say something like, "I will never remarry. I trained one, and I'm not going to train another one."

The rebuttal to that by the other spouse sometimes is, "I had to endure training by one, and I'm not going to do that again."

So, there is a little fun and humor mixed into the conversation. These pseudo-humorous comments buy time before addressing the seriousness of the matter. Today, people are getting remarried in their 70s, 80s, and even their 90s.

How does this look in practice? Let me introduce you to Stan and Betsy. They have been married 36 years and have two children. This family will be with us throughout the book.

Assume Stan and Betsy own assets together and intend those assets to be used for one another during their joint lifetime, then distributed to their two children. What happens to that plan if Stan passes away and Betsy later marries Joe?

What happens if Joe convinces Betsy that the assets she and Stan created together should be titled jointly in Betsy and Joe's name? What happens with jointly-owned property with rights of survivorship if Betsy predeceases Joe? At Joe's death, do you think he will return Betsy's money to her children?

What happens to the inheritance of Stan and Betsy's children? Seeing your hard-earned money go to someone else's family is a big concern for most people.

Another concern people worry about is that predators and creditors might take advantage of them through scams and other financial shenanigans. They are concerned that their children may not be financially mature enough to inherit their money and prudently take care of their inheritance.

Our clients express considerable concern about the possibility of family discord. It is a more significant concern for some families than others. My experience tells me that when families leave this concern to chance, it increases this risk considerably.

Then, we have concerns created by the current coronavirus pandemic. That's creating additional uncertainty and tension within the estate planning conversation.

Those are a few of the major concerns that I hear expressed. There are more. With all of these concerns, people resist or stop planning. It's an excuse to avoid having the estate planning conversation.

Procrastination - the Enemy of Effective Estate Planning

It is essential to realize that blind spots, biases, and how things occur to us influence us far more than we realize.

When those concepts weigh on us, we will likely shut down and fail to complete a plan. We call it procrastination. Procrastination is a decision. Like any decision, it expresses clarity about your intentions. It is almost a surefire way to become an estate planning victim.

By procrastinating, we have added a degree of risk to our lives and our children's lives. You and your family remain exposed.

Being more aware of blind spots, biases, and how events or situations occur allows us to muzzle that little guy on our shoulder who is constantly chattering in our ear. It will add to your knowledge, clarify points of confusion and give you a sense of confidence to move forward with your plan. Understanding what holds us back helps us we can re-write our script and focus on intention, action, and the importance of "now," regardless of what we have attempted in the past.

Virtually everyone I talk to says they never want to be a burden to their children. Blind spots, biases, and how situations occur to us can defeat that intention. I aim to change that. I stand for the proposition that you can move What You Don't Know into the What You Know category. I believe you are now more aware of how confirmation bias and cognitive dissonance can misdirect effective decision-making. I know you can better set aside the ongoing chatter you hear and use declarations to identify what you want to accomplish, how you will proceed, and set a date for completion.

If you are still with me, perhaps you have overcome blind spots, cognitive dissonance, confirmation bias, and other mental prisons that lead to procrastination. Let's start talking about a few estate planning basics with that in mind.

What Is An Estate?

S ome of you may know how famous football coach Vince Lombardi started every summer practice session, even after his Green Bay Packers had won the previous NFL Championship or Super Bowls.

"Gentlemen, this is a football."

Lombardi was a stickler for the fundamentals. That's a good starting point for us, so now a few basics. To understand estate planning, we start by asking, "What is an estate?"

Here are two acronyms I need to identify. The Internal Revenue Code will be identified as "IRC" throughout the book. The Internal Revenue Service will be identified as the "IRS."

We begin by identifying every asset the IRC says will be included in your estate for purposes of calculating your estate tax liability. The language in the IRC states:

"The value of the gross estate of the decedent shall be determined by including to the extent provided for in this part, the value at the time of his death of all property, real or personal, tangible or intangible, wherever situated."

This is somewhat technical, but it shows how the IRC extends its reach beyond what we usually consider ownership of an asset. There are relationships with assets that trigger inclusion in our taxable estate. Paraphrasing various IRC sections, we find assets are also includible in your gross estate if you:

- Have an ownership interest in the asset.
- Gifted an asset to someone within three years before your death.
- Possess a retained interest (example: a life estate interest, right to income or enjoyment).
- Make a revocable transfer of assets (example: your revocable trust assets).
- Own an annuity.
- Own property jointly with another.
- Have the power to direct or appoint an asset to a third party.
- Own life insurance on your life.

Your estate is a collection of all your assets. Plain and simple, it's everything you own, control, give away and retain an interest in, or have the power to give away.

These are common assets that we consider when determining what is in our estate for most of us.

- Checking, savings, and money market accounts in a bank, credit union, or other financial institutions.
- Investments including stocks, bonds, mutual funds, and brokerage accounts.
- Retirement accounts such as your IRAs, 401(k), 403(b), and 457 deferred compensation account.

- Real estate including your residence, vacation home, investment properties, farm and ranch land.
- Mineral interests.
- Your interest in privately-owned partnerships and corporations, including privately owned businesses.
- The value of assets you either control or have the right to control, and;
- Untitled personal property assets like your silver, china, jewelry, stamp collection, artwork, boat, farm equipment and machinery, growing crops, crops in storage, and the "stuff" inside your home.

These assets are part of your estate.

Proper estate planning includes deciding how you want your assets managed during your disability or after your death, protecting your assets from litigation, and how and when you want your estate distributed to your heirs following your death. In summary:

How will your assets be positioned and used to protect you during your lifetime?

How will your estate be distributed with the least cost and as quickly as possible after your death?

When should your beneficiaries receive your estate?

Who will manage this process?

What professional assistance is required?

You may think your estate doesn't amount to much. People frequently say, "Our estate is pretty simple" or "I don't have much." Then I find out something entirely different. Yet I have found the most vicious family disputes often center around the family armoire or heirlooms rather than the money or assets with more significant value.

Three other categories of often-overlooked assets are included in your estate.

The first would be all your retirement accounts: IRAs, 401 K's, 457's, 403 B's. Those are all included in your estate. Don't forget your Roth IRA accounts. The total value of the Roth account is included in your estate for estate tax purposes.

The second often overlooked asset is annuities. The value of the annuity at your death is included in your estate. And, keep in mind, when your beneficiaries inherit the annuity, they will pay tax on its date of death value less your initial investment. That is often a surprise.

The third often overlooked asset category is life insurance. Many are surprised to discover the policy's full death benefit value is included in your estate, not the cash value.

Estate planning is all about understanding what you own, how the asset is titled, and creating a plan to protect those assets. The plan must clearly state your wishes. It must first clarify the care you want during life. Second, it must address how you want your assets distributed to your children or your heirs in an orderly fashion with the least cost, least amount of court interference, and the least possible tax liability.

Now we turn to an overview of the role valuation plays in estate planning and its importance.

The Role of Valuation
in Estate Planning

The assets you own at the time of your death comprise your estate and are considered your gross estate for gift and estate tax purposes. According to the IRC, various regulations, private letter rulings, and case law your assets are valued at their fair market value for calculating the estate tax. The fair market value of your gross estate less debt equals your taxable estate. Estate tax rates set by the law at your death are applied to your taxable estate to determine the amount of estate tax owed.

A properly designed plan considers every asset you own or control, how each asset is titled, its fair market value when you create the plan, and the estimated value at the time of your death.

Fair market value is what a willing buyer and a willing seller would pay for the asset, assuming no undue influence or outside influence. It is the value two people with complete information and acting freely would place on an asset when offered an opportunity to exchange it for money.

Determining the fair market value has led to many legal challenges and responses from the IRS and various courts. The battles usually center on the IRS's belief that assets reported on a Form 706 U.S. Federal Estate Tax return were undervalued. The values the IRS considers undervalued typically occur due to a client implementing an advanced estate tax planning strategy that creates a discount in the fair market value of an asset includible in the estate.

Most of my clients tend to underestimate the value of their estate. I hear them say, "Well, 23 years ago, when I bought this property, I paid $40,000 for it." What you paid for the property does not affect the fair market value today. They also quickly add, "I wouldn't take that for it today." Now we are headed for the truth.

From an estate tax point of view, in determining the fair market value of an asset, the IRS always applies the "willing buyer-willing seller" test as the standard to calculate the fair market value of your gross estate. The determination is straightforward when valuing bank accounts, CDs, money market accounts, publicly traded securities, life insurance, annuities, and retirement accounts. It becomes more complicated when valuing a closely held business or farm and ranch operation. If proper advanced planning strategies are in place, it is possible to discount the gross estate value of an asset or pool of assets and reduce your tax liability.

Establishing an asset's value is also important for determining possible income tax and capital gains tax liability for your heirs. When settling an estate, we want to determine the fair market value of all assets at the time of your death. Doing so can save your heirs a considerable amount of money when they decide to sell an inherited asset in the future. We discuss this in later chapters.

To this point in the book, we have discussed who should create an estate plan, what holds us back from doing what is suitable for ourselves and our family, what an estate consists of, and why considering the value of our assets is essential.

Now it is time to explore your estate planning options.

Your Estate Planning Options

The estate planning journey usually begins with a conversation. Hopefully, with a qualified estate planning attorney. Earlier, I briefly introduced you to Stan and Betsy. For the balance of the book, we will weave a variety of estate planning situations in and around the lives of this purely hypothetical couple. We will tell the estate planning story through them. We will identify the issues and apply possible solutions to their situation.

Here's what we know about Stan and Betsy. As I mentioned, Stan and Betsy have been married for 36 years. Neither has been previously married. The principles we discuss in the book will apply regardless of marital status. They apply to anyone, whether single, married, widowed, or divorced. Everyone needs a plan.

Stan and Betsy have two children, Susan and John. Susan is 35, a successful CPA, and financially mature. She is in an "iffy" marriage to Jason. They have two children of their own.

John is another matter. He is 26, lives in California, is trying to make it in the entertainment field. He is single, unsettled, and is not financially responsible. When he calls Stan and Betsy, his last sentence

is, "...love you mom and dad. By the way, can you send more
"   ???   ."

You are correct - more money.

Now that we know our family, we need information about their
assets. We discover the following:

Asset	How titled?	Value?
Residence	Jointly	$300,000
Investment accounts	Jointly	$200,000
Retirement accounts	Individually owned	$250,000
Life insurance	On Stan	$100,000
	On Betsy	$ 20,000
Checking accounts	Individual and joint ownership	$ 30,000
Stan's business – owned 50-50 with a partner	Stan	$500,000
Stan's inheritance – an out of state farm	50-50 with Stan and his brother, individually	$250,000
Total		$1,650,000

Stan and Betsy have worked hard and have no debt, other than
routine monthly credit card bills they pay in full. Their estate value
totals $1.65 million.

Note: Let me repeat this. The strategies and tools you choose to
implement your estate plan have little to do with how much money you

have. Some readers will look at Stan and Betsy's situation and conclude estate planning must be for "wealthy" people. Some readers with $10 million will say, this doesn't apply to me. Drawing those conclusions would be a mistake. Stay with me. Focus on the principles of planning, not the value of the estate. The value of an estate will matter when planning for estate tax purposes. On other estate planning issues, the size of the estate is less relevant.

> **What is important is that you address what you want to happen at each stage of your life and ensure those objectives are clearly set forth in a well-designed estate plan.**

What happens when you decide to meet with an attorney to discuss your estate planning options? For purposes of this chapter, let's assume Stan and Betsy want to know more about estate planning in general, the steps required to complete a plan, and what to expect from the law firm.

Before the meeting, the law firm should have prepped Stan and Betsy with information and outlined issues that will be discussed so the time spent with the attorney can be most productive.

When the consultation starts, we will develop a framework for our discussion. That means we organize our time around an agenda. We confirm a few facts and have an agreement on the direction of the meeting. My mindset is first to seek understanding about their family situation. In other words, we need a clear picture of their current situation, their concerns, and what prior planning they may have completed. If they have no plan, what has been holding them back, and what are the consequences of not having a plan in place. Like a doctor, diagnosis precedes prescription.

Next, we will identify their current situation and points of concern. Call it their "As Is" situation. We may discuss delicate topics, such as a fractured relationship with a child, drug addiction, spendthrift issues, a poor relationship with a son-in-law, or creditor issues they may have, to name a few. Some may center around concerns we discussed earlier. Once we understand those concerns, what they have done about them up to this point, how long they have wrestled with them, and the implications if left unaddressed, we can move forward.

We then turn to help them identify their goals – precisely what they would like to happen at different stages in their lifetime and, of course, at their death. Think of it as Stan and Betsy's "Should Be."

Once the diagnosis is complete, we can move to the design phase. We begin identifying possible actions and solutions that will transform their situation from their existing As Is to their desired Should Be. In that discussion, hints of solutions start to appear. The design of an estate plan begins to emerge.

Stan and Betsy's Objectives

Like all of us, Stan and Betsy want to pass on their hard-earned wealth without government or court interference. Anytime our estate plan is required to endure a maze of court hearings or government issues, it dramatically slows the settlement of the estate. The current pandemic has only exacerbated these delays.

They also want to avoid paying unnecessary taxes and fees in settling their estate. I use the word "unnecessary" because, much like the example I provided earlier, failing to consider the tax implications of your plan may mean that your family pays more in taxes than they are legally obligated to pay. Depending on the law at your death, this could mean tens, perhaps hundreds, of thousands of dollars of unnecessarily paid taxes. That is not acceptable.

At this point, another objective appears. Stan and Betsy want to avoid exposing their assets to the ravaging costs of long-term care. In other words, the cost of time spent in a nursing home or on at-home care. I ask them if they have long-term health care insurance to cover nursing home expenses if needed. Of course, they both say, "I'm not going into a nursing home!" We all say that. Yet we know a significant percentage of us will have a nursing home experience.

Betsy says they have no coverage. When I ask how they intend to pay for the cost of long-term care, either one may respond, "Won't Medicare pay for it?" No, with minor exceptions. Clients are increasingly asking what steps they can take to avoid going broke from nursing homes and other crushing long-term health care expenses. Stan and Betsy say that is an objective for them as well.

Another objective is that no one wants to leave their estate structured so that their assets, surviving spouse, or family members are more vulnerable to predators and creditors. Today, scam artists boldly attack everyone, especially our most vulnerable. Deflecting and defeating scam artists is an asset protection discussion.

We then turn the conversation to their specific family situation.

The first thing they say is…

"We do not want to be a burden to our family."

Good planning will help avoid that. This desire leads to a discussion about the state of relationships within the family. What's going on? Describe the relationship you have with each of your children. With their spouses. Do your children get along? Do their spouses? How does this show up at family gatherings? Tell me more. Tell me even more. Getting truth on the table will impact decisions Stan and Betsy make about their estate plan.

No one wants their estate plan to be a source of disagreement, discontent, anger, or hostility between and among family members. No one wants family members fighting over money or personal possessions. No one likes the settlement of their estate to end what might have previously been excellent relationships permanently. We hope this would be a time of grief and gratitude where family members come closer together rather than being ripped asunder. Although a bit tender, understanding the family dynamic is vital to designing a workable plan.

Another overlooked, often unspoken objective is that people want to be remembered for more than their money. Your money may be the least important asset you leave your family.

Far more valuable is for you to document and share your life's story, your experiences – good and bad – with future generations. Share what you learned from each experience, what you stood for as a human being, and the wisdom you assimilated during your lifetime.

Taking this step will leave a genuine legacy far beyond having your name appear in a box on a family tree. Documenting and sharing your life experience offers the potential to change someone's life in your family tree in a more profound way than the money they may inherit from you.

After learning about Stan and Betsy's situation – what plans they currently have in place, their assets, their family, their concerns, and their objectives – we begin our conversation about possible options.

The Spend It All Strategy

When reviewing their options, we start by telling Stan and Betsy they could just spend everything they have and forget about estate planning. Let's get this first option out of the way. Would you want to draw your last check and last breath on the same day? That triggers a chuckle from all of us. Depleting our estate is not a realistic option. No one – no one today – wants to outlive their money. We all live longer and worry about having enough financial resources to last us into our late 80s, 90s, or beyond.

A few years ago, I remembered seeing a bumper sticker on an old lime green, beat-up Volkswagen, desperately needing a paint job. The bumper sticker was a little bit faded. The adhesive had weakened on the corners of the sticker, causing them to roll up and off the bumper. Yet, the message was clear. It said, ***"This Is My Children's Inheritance."***

That couple made an intentional decision about what their estate plan was going to be, right? Their message was clear. They were living their life to the fullest. Their estate plan was to draw their last check and last breath on the same day.

Most of us choose another path, and for a good reason. As a practical matter, everyone knows the risk and challenges of the ever-rising cost of living and the potential of having nursing home expenses devastate our estate.

The "spend it all" option is off the table because nobody wants to run out of money before running out of life. So, we will close the door on the Spend It All strategy.

The No Plan Plan

If Stan and Betsy have a No Plan Plan, we can assure them a ready-made backup plan is awaiting their family. The family will not like it, but a plan is in place. What does that mean?

Just be clear that with a No Plan Plan, the state you reside in has a plan for you. It's called the law of intestate succession.

If you have no will or no plan, each state will distribute your assets according to its own rules, the intestate succession laws. You would not like the one-size-fits-all plan the state creates for you. In most states, if you and your spouse have children and one spouse dies, the surviving spouse does not receive 100% of the estate. The outcome becomes even more complicated if you have multiple marriages with children by an earlier marriage. No thinking person wants the state dictating how their assets will be distributed.

Assets distributed according to the laws of intestate succession will require a death probate. The No Plan Plan also means no one has the legal authority to act for you or care for you if you become disabled during your lifetime.

The Last Will Plan

Next, we might talk to Stan and Betsy about utilizing a Last Will as the foundation of their estate plan. It is not unusual for people to structure the Will as what is sometimes referred to as an "I Love You" will.

For example, Stan's Will would say, "I, Stan, leave everything to Betsy, if living, and if not, to our children in equal shares, outright and free of trust."

Betsy's Will would say, "I, Betsy, leave everything to Stan, if living, and if not, to our children in equal shares, outright and free of trust."

Years ago, a Last Will was the foundation of an estate plan. Not so today.

Like assets distributed according to the laws of intestate succession, assets distributed according to a Last Will require a death probate. Where does that leave us?

Consequences of a Last Will or the No Plan Plan

For a moment, assume that during our conversation with Stan and Betsy, we discover that they each executed a traditional "I Love You" will fifteen years ago. That is the extent of their planning. After a thorough discussion and formulating a design that addresses their concerns and reaches their objectives, I ask them what they would like to do. They decide to "think it over" and not make any changes or updates at this point.

One quick point. Some of you are single. Perhaps you lost a spouse. Perhaps you never married. Perhaps you are divorced. Follow on. The principles that follow apply to those of you who are single or married.

There is one more concept we should mention. It is an oft-used workaround used to solve an estate planning issue. The question is always, "How can I transfer property to my children (or intended beneficiary) without dealing with an attorney and spending the money?" Perhaps.

There may be drawbacks, so let's explore this strategy.

Joint Tenancy

At some point, either Stan or Betsy might say, why can't we just own all of our assets jointly and let that be the extent of our planning?

They can. But, is this a good strategy? Now we review the concept of joint tenancy as an estate planning strategy.

We should be clear about what we mean by joint tenancy. There is joint tenancy with rights of survivorship, joint tenancy as tenants-in-common, and joint tenancy by the entireties.

With any joint tenancy ownership of an asset, you always have two or more people appearing on the title to the property. If the joint tenancy includes rights of survivorship ("JTWROS"), ownership automatically transfers to the surviving joint tenant by operation of law when one joint tenant dies.

In most states, the only action required is to execute an Affidavit of Surviving Joint Tenant and file it in the county where the surviving joint tenant owns real property or mineral interests. Financial vendors, such as banks or brokerage companies may require the affidavit to convert a jointly owned account into an account owned solely by the surviving joint tenant. The transfer of JTWROS property to the survivor occurs by operation of law and requires no probate.

That makes JTWROS ownership sound appealing. It is undoubtedly very seductive on the front end because we avoid the probate process on the first death. The problem is that the minute the first joint tenant dies, there is only one name on the title to the asset.

I will quickly reference a topic covered in detail in a later chapter. I refer to it as The Rule. It states that all property titled in one person's name goes through probate. Immediately upon the death of the first joint tenant, that means that property is now subject to probate.

Once people realize how JTWROS works, in an attempt to avoid hiring a lawyer to create an estate plan, an unmarried person will often attempt to avoid probate upon their death by adding children to their assets or financial accounts. Sounds simple and easy, right?

Not so fast. An experienced estate planning attorney helps with your planning by ensuring clear thinking. The minute you add a child to your accounts or deeds, you have exposed your assets to the claims of your child's creditors. And, upon your death, the surviving child owns 100% of the asset, no questions asked.

If your objective is to leave your estate to your children in equal shares, yet you only add one child's name to your asset as a joint tenant, will your children receive an equal share of your estate? Probably not. I hear people say, "I'm not worried. I know Susie will split everything equally with her brother and sister". And candles light themselves, right?

Joint tenancy can also create unfavorable tax issues, especially when adding children's names to assets with significant value. When a child's name is on your real estate, your son must join in the conveyance if you wish to sell the land. Even more troubling is that his spouse must also sign off on the conveyance. Most people do not want to be required to get their son or daughter-in-law's permission to sell their home.

Another method of joint ownership is joint tenants in common ("JTIC"). An asset titled JTIC property is individually owned property. Once again, we encounter The Rule. Your share of the JTIC interest is required to go through probate.

Joint tenancies by the entireties ("JTBE") is a concept recognized in some but not all states. It operates the same as joint tenancy with survivorship. However, creditor protection features are available to spouses who own an asset JTBE that are not available to the normal survivorship joint tenancy.

In sum, joint tenancy ownership is seductive at the onset and potentially disastrous on the backend. We recommend joint tenancy ownership not be utilized as the centerpiece of an effective estate plan for those reasons. There is another significant reason looming out there.

The Grand Canyon Exposure Point

Using joint tenancy or a Last Will as the foundation of your estate plan also leaves you vulnerable to issues around lifecare planning options. What happens if you become incapacitated? Who has the legal authority to act on your behalf? Will a Living Probate – guardianship or conservatorship – be required to resolve those issues? Does it make sense to leave yourself exposed to that?

The choice to Do Nothing, use a Last Will, or use joint tenancy as the foundation of your estate plan will transfer assets to your heirs upon your death. Do those strategies help if you become incapacitated?

No. Those options do not protect you in that situation. The Last Will only becomes effective after your death, long after you may have become incapacitated. None of those options provide lifecare planning, ensuring someone has the legal authority to act on your behalf if you are incapacitated. In the absence of closing this Grand Canyon Exposure Point, someone may have to open a Living Probate – a guardianship or conservatorship – on your behalf.

Guardianship (care of the person) and Conservatorship (care of the person's property) are court-administered proceedings designed to protect someone if they are incapacitated, can no longer care for themselves, and have not created a lifecare plan to protect themselves.

A Living Probate proceeding is a nightmarish experience for families. It is humiliating, time-consuming, expensive, and leaves the court in control of your assets. Think about this. How would you like to have to hire our firm to help you prepare a detailed description of your finances and how you plan to care for your spouse, go to court, stand before the judge and get their approval to spend your own money for the care and well-being of your spouse?

Does it make sense to leave yourself exposed to that?

A Last Will or using joint tenancy will not address the health or medical needs during your lifetime, especially if you become incapacitated. More is needed, so we shift our conversation to Life Care planning as a component of an effective estate plan. Let's have a look.

Aligning Life Planning and Estate Planning

It is critical to integrate life planning into your estate plan. By life planning, I mean addressing the health risks we encounter during our lifetime and making decisions about the type of care you want and who will make decisions for you if you cannot make them yourself.

To have a comprehensive plan, you must declare your intention on these issues. It does not happen by default. It is important because the odds of you becoming disabled are greater than you dying. No one wants to be a burden to their children, right?

It is as essential to plan for lifetime contingencies as it is to prepare for the distribution of your estate. And life-care planning extends beyond your health to include careful consideration of your investments. Ignore that statement at your peril.

This last point is one reason we took advantage of my experience in the investment management business and created a sister firm to the law firm that is a registered investment advisory firm. Its purpose is to help our clients with retirement planning and investment management. Our approach is comprehensive "wealth management" from a legal and financial perspective. Clients who work with our legal and financial team ensure they have a plan offering asset protection from numerous risk points and potential liabilities during their lifetime.

For example, if you become disabled, you surely want documents in place authorizing specific people to act on your behalf and take care of you. Incurring a disability without the proper legal documentation that authorizes someone to act on your behalf can be disastrous. Failing to see the importance of having this protection is what we all a blind spot.

Let us apply these concepts to Stan and Betsy. Remember, the only plan they have in place is a Last Will executed years ago. I am sitting in my office when their daughter, Susan Jones, calls. I pick up the phone. Susan tells me Stan is in the hospital. She says she knows her mom and dad met with me to update their plan a few months earlier and would like to know about Stan's health care documents.

Although Stan and Betsy would have to permit me to discuss the details of their plan with her, I can let her know her parents did not retain us to do any work for them at that time. All I can share is that her parents told us they have an old Last Will. Susan's response? Oh, no.

Susan informs me Stan has had a stroke and is in the hospital. I later discovered Stan's condition quickly deteriorated. He is on the verge of being disabled.

The critical question is: what legal authority does Betsy have to act on Stan's behalf? Does the fact Stan and Betsy are married give her legal authority to act on his behalf?

Sooner or later, Betsy is going to run into a problem. She will find that she has no legal authority to act on Stan's behalf in many situations.

She might have joint signing authority on a bank account, maybe even a brokerage account. But if Betsy wishes to make changes or make modifications to an insurance policy, a retirement plan, or any asset that might be titled in Stan's name alone, she will have an issue.

Stan and Betsy's current plan fails to create any legal authority for them to act on behalf of the other if a disability occurs. The only way for that authority to be granted at this point is to open a living probate, sometimes called guardianship or conservatorship.

What is a Living Probate?

A living probate is a court proceeding created to appoint someone to handle the personal and financial affairs of someone who can no longer act on their own behalf.

More specifically, a conservatorship is when a judge appoints a responsible person or organization (called the "conservator") to manage the financial assets of someone who cannot manage their own finances.

A guardianship is a court appointment authorizing a person to act, care for, and make personal decisions on behalf of an adult with incapacity. The incapacitated person is referred to as a "ward" of the state.

Anyone with interest can make an application for a conservatorship or guardianship order. Either can be voluntary agreements, but that is often not the case.

One challenge with a living probate proceeding is that it can be a "forced" proceeding. In other words, the person who is allegedly unable to manage their affairs may have a very different opinion about their condition. They may resist efforts by others – often family members – seeking to establish guardianship for their personal matters or a conservator to oversee and handle their financial affairs.

Perhaps you have read about Britney Spears, a famous American songwriter-singer. After a very public breakdown a decade ago, Britney entered a voluntary conservatorship with her father, Jamie Spears. Under the conservatorship terms, Jamie has complete control over Britney's financial and medical affairs.

Now, Ms. Spears is asserting she has lost complete control over her life, and the court supervision over her life needs to end. She is "required" to work, and that work generates millions of dollars of income each year. To illustrate the extent of the control, Britney is prohibited from removing a diaphragm that keeps her from having more children. Her mandated work provides financial support for her father and those who work for her.

Britney has now successfully concluded her challenge to a court-appointed conservator controlling her personal and financial life. In June 2021, Ms. Spears spoke openly for herself in her conservatorship case. The court proceedings were live-streamed, giving the public a glimpse into the singer's perspective and experience for the last 13 years. For the first time, Britney spoke publicly about her mental health struggles, forced work, loss of control of her life, and why her conservatorship should be ended. Her situation spawned a *#FreeBritney* movement. There was a White House petition filed supporting her release from court control.

What was once a voluntary understanding was later on a forced arrangement by the court. Because of her victory, she is now free of that control. Many living probates are forced proceedings and often cause irreparable damage to family relationships.

Now imagine. What is the condition of relationships within the Spears family?

Back to Stan and Betsy. Knowing what we know about Stan's declining health and what Betsy is now facing, does it make sense to declare your intention regarding your lifetime care choices and avoid all of this?

Or would you prefer to have to hire me, go to court, stand in front of a judge, who you probably don't know, and ask that judge's permission to spend your money on the care and well-being of your own spouse?

While the reason the law provides for a living probate is well-intended, you would find the experience humiliating, time-consuming, frustrating, and expensive. We also know from the experience of Britney Spears that once a court establishes a living probate, it is not the easiest legal arrangement to terminate.

Here is reality. People do become incapacitated like Stan in our case study. So, some instances require a living probate – a guardianship, perhaps a conservatorship. Sometimes the two are combined. Leaving it entirely up to a judge to decide who should oversee you personally or who should be appointed to handle your financial affairs is not a very good option. Yet, this is people's exposure if they fail to create a disability plan as part of their estate plan. It is better to declare your preferences in the appropriate legal document as part of a comprehensive estate plan.

What happens if Stan does not recapacitate. What happens if his disability continues to worsen each day? What happens if his condition continues? Unless he recapacitates, Stan's living probate – conservatorship and guardianship – will continue until his death.

At the time of Stan's death, any asset titled in his name will have to go through another legal proceeding, the legal proceeding Norman Dacey advised us to avoid - death probate. That leads me to a rule that readers should thoroughly understand.

What is The Rule, and how does it influence our estate planning decisions?

What is The Problem With Death Probate?

The Rule states that all assets titled in your individual name have to go through probate. Let that soak in for a minute. I briefly mentioned The Rule in the chapter on joint tenancy. Those assets will go through the probate process and will either be distributed to your heirs according to your Last Will or, if you do not have a Last Will, according to the laws of intestate succession the state created for you.

> **The Rule: all assets titled in an individual's name must go through probate.**

Death probate is a legal proceeding designed to do for us what we can no longer do ourselves. We have passed on. We might want our home to go to our spouse, certain assets to our children, or perhaps smaller gifts to our favorite niece, church, or charity.

But, after our passing, we can no longer sign the deed transferring ownership of our real estate – or minerals - to our intended beneficiaries. We can no longer execute assignments of financial assets, contracts, or leases that will effectively transfer ownership to our beneficiaries. We have no way to settle our debts.

The legal system has a court-directed process to make these transfers for us. It is called probate–death probate.

When a death probate is opened, the court appoints an executor referred to as a personal representative in many jurisdictions. The court issues Letters Testamentary naming the personal representative and authorizing them to act on behalf of the deceased's estate. In effect, the personal representative becomes the authorized agent of the court for the estate of the deceased. They have statutory duties they must carry out and other duties they will exercise based on the type of assets owned and the size of the estate.

Among the statutory requirements is publishing a notice to creditors to determine if the deceased owed money to any third party. The personal representative will - unless granted an exception - within two (2) months after the issuance of his letters, file notice with the creditors of the decedent and publish in a newspaper where the probate is occurring a notice to unknown, possible creditors to file their claims with the court. This open period typically runs for 90-120 days, depending on each state's law. The claims against the deceased will be forever barred unless presented to the personal representative by the presentment date stated in the notice.

While this is occurring, the personal representative's responsibilities are piling up. Their first step will be retaining an attorney to help them navigate the probate process. Many personal representatives have busy lives of their own. On top of their busy lives, you have just given them a J-O-B by naming someone your personal representative!

The attorney will help the personal representative understand the decedent's Last Will, or if there was no Will, acquaint them with the state's laws of intestate succession. They will identify beneficiaries of the estate and how assets are to be distributed to each beneficiary.

Legal counsel will also help develop the checklist of all actions required to complete the probate. The personal representative will often retain an attorney to act as their back office and complete all the details needed to complete the probate process successfully.

Another critical action is meeting with the deceased's beneficiaries, often the deceased's spouse, if living and, if not, the children. One of the children may be appointed to serve as the personal representative. Or, two children may be appointed as co-personal representatives. That decision alone can trigger a variety of issues. Not all are positive.

Following their official court appointment, the personal representative works to identify all assets owned by the deceased and identify all known liabilities so they can respond to creditor claims as they appear. Once assets are identified, the personal representative will confirm the deceased's ownership. They will share the Letters Testamentary with the financial vendor or other interested parties who may require proof of the personal representative's power to act on behalf of the estate.

After compiling an accurate asset list, the personal representative will want to establish a date of death value for assets owned by the estate. Determining the date of death valuations is critical to establishing what is referred to as a step-up in the asset's tax basis to its fair market value at the decedent's death. Based on current law, adjusting asset values up to the fair market value at the time of death means that heirs of the deceased will pay taxes only on any appreciation that occurs between the date of death and the date of their sale. The total accrued capital gains tax the deceased would have paid if he sold the asset during his lifetime is eliminated.

During the probate, the personal representative is responsible for tax reporting. There will be a final 1040 filed on April 15th in the year following the deceased's death. Between the date of death and the estate's closing, the personal representative will also file a 1041 Fiduciary Return to account for the estate's tax liability between the date of death and the estate's final settlement.

Suppose the decedent is a business owner, a partner in a business, or owns investment properties, minerals, or more complicated assets. In that case, the personal representative's job becomes much more difficult and time-consuming.

Probate also serves as a place where disputes are resolved. If family members contest the provisions of the Last Will or seek to render the Last Will null and void, the probate court is the forum where the Will contest takes place. It does not require much imagination to see that death probate is a fertile field for family disputes.

Nothing good comes from a probate estate settlement that drags on for months and months. Some probates last for years. It converts hairline fractures within family units into compound fractures, often ending what was a workable, if not great, relationship. It can sever great relationships between and among siblings. As I said, family discord can grow prolifically in the fertile field of a probate proceeding.

Norman Dacey's book *How to Avoid Probate* revealed why people dislike probate. My personal and professional experience confirms his account. Here are a few reasons.

Time

The first reason to avoid probate is the time required to complete the process. Many of the probate timelines are set by statutory obligations, some of which I mentioned earlier. We have no control over those.

People do not like the time delays that accompany a probate proceeding. Probate takes too long. It is not uncommon for probate to last from 12 to 18 months. Some probates have lasted over 30 years— for example, the probate of Howard Hughes. You could have entered kindergarten, continued through your senior year, received your high school diploma, and Elvis Presley's probate would have still been open.

The annals of the probate contain nightmarish experiences of families who have seen their loved one's probate take far too long to settle.

Expense

Secondly, people are concerned about the cost of probate.

It is not unusual for probate to cost anywhere from three to seven percent of the estate's gross value. That can add up to a significant amount of money. When speaking to a group in a smaller county seat community early in my career, I would visit the county courthouse over the lunch hour. I spent that hour combing through randomly selected probate records. I made copies and would show them to clients so they could see the reality of a probate experience.

I remember one probate record I reviewed in a small county seat community courthouse. The total value of the estate was $326,000. The Final Decree was 14 pages long, single-spaced on 8x14 inch legal-sized paper. In addition to her home, two bank accounts, a car, and personal belongings, the asset list consisted of items like "One lot old milk cans, one 6-foot aluminum ladder, one well-preserved saddle...." The list of similar items went on and on. The legal fee was $26,000. Seriously.

Publicity

The third issue is that probate is a matter of public record. Anyone can walk into a courthouse, open your probate file, and examine every detail about your financial affairs. Through the years, I have spent many hours going into county courthouses and scouring through probate records to discover what lessons I could learn from those who fell victim to The Rule.

Your probate record is an open book. You might be wondering, "Why should I care? I'm gone." Suppose you are a business owner or have a farm and ranch operation, and the operation continues after your death. In that case, you might not want the details of your financial life exposed to competitors, lenders, or vendors. If you have a bank loan, according to the promissory note you signed, your death will likely be treated as "an event of default." That alone will create significant tension.

A few years ago, we handled a probate for a business owner in Missouri. Before his death, our client was attempting to sell his business to a competitor in the same community. When the probate records were made public, the competitor had access to previously private financial information about our client's business. In subsequent negotiations, the potential buyer used that information against our client's estate. Most people do not want their entire financial life laid out for public consumption.

Multiple Probates

Adding to those reasons, your estate might be subject to an ancillary probate. In layman's terms, it means multiple probates. Suppose that at your death, you own property in another state. You will likely have to endure two probates – one in your state of residence; the other in the state where the property is located. When probate is required for an out-of-state asset, it is referred to as an ancillary probate.

Ancillary probates occur for a variety of reasons. You may reside in one state and own minerals inherited from your parents in another. We often find mineral interests have not been cleared – brought up to date through multiple generations – for many years. A succeeding generation decides the interest is too small to worry about, and the minerals are not producing. Then a well is leased, then drilled, and successfully completed. When the oil or gas starts flowing, and revenue occurs, it can change a family's financial fortune. At that point, it is costly to clean up the title and receive the benefits.

Ancillary probates occur if you inherit real property – say a family farm – with a sibling or any third party—a brother. Ownership will typically be titled as joint tenants in common in each of your names. As we mentioned in an earlier chapter, this produces a different result than owning the property as joint tenants with rights of survivorship.

When an asset is owned jointly with rights of survivorship, there is no probate following the first death, except a simple filing of an Affidavit of Surviving Joint Tenant, or similar document. By contrast, tenants in common ownership is an individually owned property. Upon your demise, your interest transfers to your heirs. That interest is subject to The Rule, thus triggering a probate, more specifically, an ancillary probate if the property is located in a state other than your residence.

Suppose you are a Missouri resident and own property in Oklahoma titled in your name. In that case, The Rule makes it likely you will have to probate in Missouri and Oklahoma, where the property is located.

> **These handicaps - time, expense, publicity, and the possibility of multiple probates – clearly demonstrate why probate should be avoided.**

We follow Norman Dacey's recommendation, confirmed by our experience, and advise our clients to avoid it. Avoiding probate is one of the many benefits of a revocable living trust.

However, if you go to an attorney in your community, they will likely suggest a Last Will and Testament because they do not want to avoid probate. Some lawyers believe differently about probate – tell you it's not that bad – and you don't need a trust. If so, rest assured probate is a significant revenue generator for their practice. Just remember the message shared by Norman Dacey.

To avoid having assets titled in our individual names and expedite the orderly and timely transfer of assets to the next generation, I have always recommended our clients use a revocable trust as the foundation of their estate plan. The revocable trust design is ideal for protecting you during your lifetime and avoiding a death probate. There is no comparison.

Estate Planning Is All About Asset Protection

Regardless of how old you are, your plan needs to be all-inclusive irrespective of where you are in life. It must consider all possibilities and clearly describe those you choose to make health care decisions for you and manage your assets when you are gone.

Be intentional. You decide what happens and when.

Start here. Every estate plan should have a goal.

Setting an estate planning goal is one of the crucial components of the estate planning conversation. The first step is to get to clarity. Clarity about the need to create the plan, clarity about what the plan will look like, and clarity about when you want the plan in place. Without intention and clarity, nothing gets done. I once heard a good friend say," If it's cloudy at the pulpit, it is foggy in the pew."

When you are clear about where you are, what is important to you, and what you want to happen at certain stages in your life, the more efficiently the attorney you work with will be able to capture those thoughts, objectives, and goals and get them committed to writing.

An experienced estate planning attorney focuses on the right questions that allow your goals, concerns, and obstacles to emerge to the surface like a sunken ship retrieved from the ocean floor for its bounty.

As an example, think about children. You may have a variety of different thoughts. What's the age of that child? If you have young children, you know it makes no sense for a ten-year-old child to inherit money. So what is going to happen to that child?

And what happens if you die and have a life insurance policy? Is that policy going to be used to pay off the mortgage on the house? Or will that money be used to set up an education trust fund to benefit a child's education?

Setting a clear goal is critical. An experienced professional will help you do that and, from that point, design a great plan.

Protection From Predators and Creditors

As mentioned earlier, estate planning is really about asset protection. We know we have exposure if we fail to plan.

The question is, what degree of asset protection do you require? Asset protection should protect you against living probate and death probate, offer liability protection to the extent necessary, and minimize estate and income taxes.

Your estate plan should identify steps to protect the estate if either Stan or Betsy decides to get remarried after the first death. You want to protect your estate from the problems that can happen when you have a second or perhaps even third marriage. Assets get retitled into the new spouse's name and inadvertently end up going to the children of that spouse rather than the children of the original couple, Stan and Betsy.

An estate plan has the potential to protect the assets from predators and creditors - not only of Stan and Betsy but of their children.

And what happens if either Stan or Betsy has to go into a nursing home?

Estate planning is really about asset protection. It's about protecting that estate and any contingencies that could occur.

Some may be thinking, "I don't need an estate plan because I don't have enough assets."

Let me just be clear about what an estate is again. An estate is anything you own. It might come in the form of stocks, bonds, mutual funds, bank accounts, brokerage accounts, everything from series e bonds to IRAs, 401 K's, but let's not forget a couple of things. Life insurance death benefits and all of your personal property are considered part of your estate. Sometimes I refer to the latter as the stuff.

So everything you own and everything you might inherit comprise your estate. Everyone has an estate.

Sometimes people say, "Well, gosh, I don't have anything worth passing on." That belief leads to why people don't plan.

People don't plan because they say, "Well, I don't have an estate, so I don't have enough to plan." Or, "Even if I did have something, I don't know what to do, because it's too hard or there are too many decisions that I have to make. And I get confused about what I hear about what proper estate planning should include."

Whether someone should have a plan depends more on what they want to happen at different stages in their life than the value of their estate or how much money they have. This is particularly true regarding the two significant issues we discussed: disability and death. And those can occur overnight.

We have had examples where people completed their estate plan, then called back a few days later, saying they needed to modify their plan. We discover their otherwise healthy, 40-year-old son was in a severe car accident over the weekend, and now he's a quadriplegic. What do we do? Again, the point is, whether it's for your care and well-being or the care and well-being of your loved ones, everyone needs a plan. That plan needs to protect your assets, regardless of the size of your estate.

Now an important question is: "Is estate planning a do-it-yourself proposition? Are online options the answer?" After the next chapter, you decide.

Can I Do This Myself?

We must address one more point before moving on. You might be wondering why you shouldn't just download documents from the internet or an online document provider and do this yourself.

Of course, you can do this yourself. You can also operate on your own heart or brain.

Estate planning is not a do-it-yourself exercise, at least any more than you would fly a Boeing 787 Dreamliner or act as your own brain surgeon.

Online options such as Legal Zoom are not very thorough. They provide generic forms, have you plug in your name, and pay an attorney a few hundred dollars to say it's legal. Legality is not the only question. A better question is whether those online forms address your specific situation, accurately identify your goals, and craft the appropriate solution.

On top of that, who will you or your family call when you have questions or need updates? Who will your family call to help them settle your estate? Will you get the same attorney? They probably won't even be in business when you need them the very most.

Do not sit down and type out your own plan. Do not go to Office Depot or another online provider, download documents and think you have created an estate plan.

You deserve the best legal expertise possible to help you through the estate planning process.

Here are a couple more items to add to the Do Not Do This list. Yes, what I am about to say may sound self-serving. Sometimes people only consider the investment required to complete a comprehensive plan and take the low-cost option. But, what is the actual "cost" of the least expensive option?

Keep this in mind. We feel our documents are free. The investment you make is based on your choices. Once we know what you want, we can apply our experience and expertise to design and implement a perfect plan for you and your family. More importantly, it means someone will be there when you need them the most, answer your questions, answer your family's questions, and implement your plan with precision.

Here's an example. Recently, a lady – let's call her Sue - was referred to us by another client. Sue is the only child of her mother, Ann. Ann is 82, healthy, and in her second marriage to Herb. Herb has four living children and has been suffering from dementia for the past couple of years. His memory is fading more rapidly each day. One of Herb's sons supported their marriage, one was neutral, and the other two were hostile to Ann and Sue from the day they exchanged vows.

During Herb and Ann's marriage, an attorney created a trust for each of them. Sue was the sole beneficiary of Ann's trust, and Herb was to serve as successor trustee for Ann's trust. As a quick reminder, the trustee has a fiduciary obligation to manage trust assets and distribute assets exactly as you outline in your plan. On a separate document, Ann indicated that with few exceptions, Sue was to receive all of her personal property – jewelry, family heirlooms, and so forth.

The trust document was one of the worst I have ever seen. In addition to poor drafting, no corresponding pour-over will was executed with the trust stipulating that Ann's trust was the beneficiary on any property titled in Ann's name that might require probate (remember The Rule?).

Some assets owned by Herb and Ann were held as separate property. Those assets were still titled in either Herb or Ann's individual names. Herb and Ann owned other assets as joint tenants with rights of survivorship. In one instance, Herb and Ann opened a joint tenancy with survivorship account with a bank in Canada. Ann contributed $208,000 to the account, and Herb contributed $40,000. With a survivorship joint tenancy account, upon the death of one joint tenant, the asset belongs to the survivor by operation of law. The account was invested in a money market account and never used. They were considering closing it.

With that in mind, a couple of months ago, Herb wrote three checks to Ann on the joint Canadian bank account totaling $200,000. Ann gave them to her daughter Sue and told her to deposit them into a joint account owned by Ann and Sue together. This amount was approximately what Ann had contributed to the original account. Sue failed to cash the checks and was still carrying them in her purse a few weeks later.

Then Ann was killed in a traffic accident.

Think about what has happened. We previously established that all assets titled in one person's name goes through probate. We advised Sue to deposit the three checks into our firm's trust account, pending resolution of the many issues we discovered. We were not surprised when the bank called Herb and asked him if he had written checks on the account. He said no.

As the surviving joint tenant, the $208,000 Ann contributed to the account was now owned by Herb. Ann's daughter, Sue, is not entitled to one dollar.

On top of that, the remaining assets titled in Ann's name required probate. But, and this is a Big But, there is no last will stating that the beneficiary of probated assets is Ann's trust. If that had happened, Sue would have received the asset as the sole beneficiary of Ann's trust.

Because there is no last will, we now have intestate probate. From Sue's point of view, the challenge is that under our state law, as a surviving spouse, Herb will receive one-half of the probated assets, and Sue will only receive the other one-half.

If this is not enough, Sue took her mom's ashes from the funeral home, intending to split them with Herb, only to discover one of his sons, who opposed the marriage from the beginning, called the police to report Sue had stolen the ashes.

What should you take from this? First, an experienced estate planning attorney could have pre-empted many of these issues. Second, you must work with a professional who knows what they are doing. Third, becoming a Do-It-Yourself attorney on these matters is fool's gold even with a modest estate. Finally, bad behavior can ruin a good plan.

Be smart about this. Otherwise, your thinking may be influenced by confirmation bias or cognitive dissonance. Seek a professional who will partner with you, collaborate with you, ask penetrating questions, create a comfortable relationship, and help you successfully navigate the straights and narrows of the estate planning process.

You cannot get what a professional advisor offers online. An estate planning pro will be there to help when you feel you are walking out on that plank alone, experiencing uncertainty, or needing to understand the implications of an important decision better. No online chat box will do that.

You do not want to go this alone. We have been forced into court to clean up so many documents through the years because people hired inexperienced, cheap attorneys or tried to do this themselves. It always turns out to be a disaster.

In this area, the cost of not using an experienced professional is exceptionally high, far higher than the investment required to do it right. You do not want your family to pay for that mistake. And you certainly do not want to pay for it yourself during your lifetime if you become incapacitated.

Find someone who can and will help you do this the right way. It is a crucial piece of the equation. *Money magazine* and Suze Orman have said that when people are looking for attorneys with estate planning expertise, they should contact members of the American Academy of Estate Planning Attorneys. You should follow their advice. To find out about an Academy member near you, go to www.aaepa.com.

We have reviewed some of the hurdles and mindsets that keep people from taking action to start and complete an effective estate plan. And we have examined what can go wrong without professional counsel.

Now we turn to the components of a comprehensive estate plan.

Putting It Together – Components of Your Plan

Designing your estate plan is a process where you declare your intentions about what happens to you and your estate if you become incapacitated or at the time of your death.

The process includes deciding who you want responsible for overseeing your instructions about what you want to occur at those times. Think about a will or a trust as tools you use within your estate planning design process to carry out those wishes.

Do I Choose A Trust Or A Will?

One decision you will make is whether you will use a last will or a revocable trust as the foundation of your plan.

We must remember a critically important distinction between a will and a trust. Yes, a will is effective when executed but only becomes operational upon death. Between the execution date and your death, it offers you no protection. It provides no life-care protection. Further, any assets distributed by your last will must go through probate.

Tradition, and the bias of probate attorneys, may make it seem like a Last Will and Testament is the end-all, be-all estate planning document. However, people should consider using a revocable trust as the foundation of their estate planning.

You would think that all lawyers would recommend using a revocable trust as the foundation of an estate plan, but that is often not the case. We often hear people tell us the attorney they spoke to said, "Probate is not that difficult in our state." Right.

This happens because probate fees are a future source of revenue for probate lawyers, almost on a guaranteed basis. Again, using a last will leaves your family exposed to probate.

You do need a last will. However, the preferred last will is referred to as a pour-over will. It works in tandem with a revocable trust.

By contrast, a revocable trust - one that you can change, modify, control, and amend or modify anytime you want - is a document that is effective and operational when executed. If properly constructed, the trust will contain provisions that protect you in the event of your disability or incapacity and at death.

Your trust will identify someone – a successor trustee – to oversee and manage assets titled in the name of the trust for your care and well-being during your lifetime.

If it is structured correctly and appropriately funded, none of your assets will go through probate. That is a tremendous advantage.

In addition, whether using a trust or a last will as the foundation of your estate plan, other tools are required to maximize protection during incapacity or disability.

Now we examine each of the estate planning tools in greater detail.

The Hub of the Spoke - The Revocable Trust

A trust is a method of owning assets during your lifetime and then transferring those assets to your intended beneficiaries with the least cost and shortest time delays.

Our firm was among the first – if not the first - in our state to almost exclusively recommend the use of a revocable trust rather than a will as the foundation of a well-constructed estate plan. Since 1986, thousands have attended or viewed our education programs on estate planning.

As you might imagine, I wasn't a very popular guy with the probate attorneys. Years earlier, after reading Norman Dacey's book, I became intensely interested in and intrigued by the benefits of using a revocable trust as the foundation of an estate plan rather than a will. It was time to put this information into action.

My curiosity led me to explore the history of trust usage and how it evolved from when it emerged during the 12th century.

Origins of the Trust

The concept of a trust originated sometime in the 12th century in the English Courts of Chancery. In those days, the English common law, a derivative of ancient Roman law, could be quite harsh in its literal interpretations and applications. Chancery Courts were created to inject an element of equity or fairness into the resolution of disputes.

The Crusades presented landowners and the courts with the challenge of deciding who would be responsible for the land's operation, care and upkeep if the King called upon its owner to fight in the Crusades and be subject to long absences due to the fighting.

At the time, The Chancery had jurisdiction over all matters of equity, including the separate legal doctrines of trusts, land law, estate administration and guardianships.

Like the Roman law before it, the English version viewed property ownership as indivisible, meaning whoever owned legal title owned all rights and privileges associated with the land. That meant what it means today. Property owners are vested with all right, title, and interests in and to their property. They can freely buy or sell full property ownership to or from others. Today, one distinction is the ability to sever ownership of the land's surface from the air and sub-surface (mineral) rights.

The Crusades required a new arrangement. When landowners became Crusaders, most did not want to sell their land. Yet, early on, the landowning Crusader would convey ownership of his lands to another to manage the estate and pay and receive feudal duties during his absence, understanding that the ownership would be transferred back to him upon returning. However, upon returning, the Crusader often encountered a refusal to return ownership of the property. What were the Crusader's options?

The frustrated Crusader's remedy was petitioning the King, who would refer the matter to his Lord Chancellor. The Lord Chancellor could decide the case according to his conscience, determining what was "equitable" or "fair." Typically, the Lord Chancellor would consider it unconscionable that the current owner could go back on his word and deny the claims of the Crusader. Therefore, he would find in favor of the returning Crusader.

Over time a solution emerged. In most cases, the Court of Chancery would look at the situation with an eye on fairness or equity and re-establish ownership in the name of the Crusader. To prevent this issue, it became standard practice for the Court to allow a third party to hold the land for the benefit of the original owner, the Crusader.

The third party would have responsibility for the land in the Crusader's absence and convey it back to him when requested. The Crusader was the "beneficiary" and the named third party land title holder the "trustee." The term "use of land" developed into what we know now as a "trust."

In modern trust law, we can create both stand-alone inter-vivos trusts created during our lifetime and testamentary trusts created after our death according to our last will. Both can determine how property is invested, owned, and distributed following our death.

A trustee is not to be confused with the owner or the beneficiary. An individual or entity can be a trustee. The trustee is responsible for carrying out the terms of the trust. They have a fiduciary duty to the trust's beneficiaries to prudently manage, invest, and deal with the property. The trustees can be liable to the beneficiaries if they violate those duties.

The trustor (sometimes referred to as the settlor or grantor) of the trust is the person who owns the property, creates the terms of the trust, and conveys money, property, or assets to the trust. In most revocable trusts created today, the trustor also serves as trustee as long as they are willing and able to serve in that role. Likewise, the trustor is also usually named the beneficiary of the trust. When a person creating a trust is named as the trustor, trustee, and beneficiary, it is equivalent to holding an outright fee simple title in the assets and property.

There are no Crusades today, as they occurred in the Middle Ages. For most of us, the primary reason for creating the revocable trust during our lifetime is to set the stage for an easy transition to oversee our assets in the event of our disability or death.

"Tomorrow" is never promised to any of us. Disability or death may occur suddenly, as it did with my father. If that happens and there is no trust, your assets are subject to either living or death probate. Perhaps, both. Hopefully, you are beginning to see that trusts are an extremely useful tool to ensure appropriate management of your assets for your benefit if you are disabled. And that prudent oversight continues until your death, so you are assured your wishes are carried out.

As you can see, using a trust for estate planning purposes is not a new phenomenon. That said, trusts were seldom used until the past 30 years or so. When I began my practice, seeing someone us a trust as the foundation of their planning was almost a novelty. Now, through education and exposure, more people are aware of the pitfalls of probate and having their assets exposed to publicity, the time it takes to complete probate, its expense, and the possibility of multiple probates.

Advantages of a Trust

The main benefit of a trust is that assets titled in the name of the trust will not be subject to The Rule and will not have to go through probate. That alone outweighs all disadvantages.

Again, the trust is going to protect you during your lifetime. A will does not create any lifetime planning for you. As I said earlier, it only springs into effect when you die. By contrast, the trust contains language authorizing the current trustee to act on your behalf and use trust assets to provide for your care if you are incapacitated.

Effective planning with a trust allows you to minimize estate tax liability. Yes, you can do that through a will. If you are married, the challenge is that achieving maximum estate tax benefits using a will requires two probates! Both estates will go through probate following the death of each spouse. That is a big disadvantage to using a will to minimize estate tax. All things considered, it is much more advantageous to implement effective estate tax planning through a trust.

Finally, the trust allows the assets titled in the name of the trust to be administered by the trustee without court supervision and control. Most people like the idea of keeping the legal system as far away as possible.

Disadvantages of a Trust

Some say a disadvantage of using a trust as the foundation of your estate plan is it takes a little more work on the part of a client to create that trust. It certainly requires more work by the attorney. Indeed, we need to spend much more time with the plan design than with the last will. The revocable trust includes features that protect you during your lifetime and at the time of death. That requires considerable discussion, much thought, and work by you and the attorney.

Second, the revocable trust may require a greater investment than setting up a will. The trust requires more detailed drafting because of the life care language and other contingencies not needed in a last will.

Third, a revocable trust will not protect your assets from the legitimate claims of your creditors. If a creditor takes a judgment against you, assets titled in the name of a revocable trust will be available to satisfy the claim. The reasoning is that because you can revoke the trust, the creditor can stand in your place, exercise revocation powers, and access the assets.

I do not view the absence of liability or lawsuit protection as a disadvantage. The last will does not offer that protection either. While the revocable trust offers many advantages that fall under my broadly defined asset protection umbrella, those who desire more advanced asset protection will use strategies and tools described later in the book.

Everyone needs the life planning tools that we talked about earlier. Those tools include the durable power of attorney for financial transactions, the healthcare power of attorney, advance directives, and HIPAA releases.

The fourth reason people balk at creating a trust is the time factor. It takes more time to complete the three steps required to create an effective revocable trust plan. There is a time requirement to meet with the attorney and decide on the design of your plan. Second, it takes time for the attorney to integrate the plan design into appropriate documents. Finally, all of your assets must be properly titled in the name of your trust. This step is vital. We link some assets to your trust with new beneficiary designations.

We call this final step funding the trust. It is a critical element of using a trust for your estate plan. The terms of the trust will only apply to those assets titled in its name. If assets remain titled in your name, The Rule applies, and probate follows. Unfortunately, we see many trusts that are not adequately funded.

Those are four reasons why people sometimes find it a little more challenging to create a trust.

Parties to the Trust

As mentioned before, there have always been three parties in a trust – trustors (sometimes referred to as grantors or settlors), trustees, and beneficiaries. Every trust created since the beginning has these three parties. How does this work in real time?

A trust is a contract. Who are the trustors? These are the people who own the property and create the plan. The second party included in every trust is the trustee. The trustee is the party that manages the assets titled in the name of the trust. The third party to the trust is the beneficiary. These are the people who get to use and enjoy the property. In other words, spend the money.

Going back to Stan and Betsy, they would appear in all three positions in the trust if they created a trust. They would appear as the trustors, because they own the property and are setting up the plan. They would appear as trustees because they want to continue to manage the trust's assets, just as they do now. Finally, because their bills will continue to come in, and they want the ability to pay their bills in a timely fashion and spend the money as they wish, they will name themselves as beneficiaries.

It's possible to set up a trust and name someone else as the initial trustee. The most common design includes the client in all three positions. The critical point here is the fact that trust is revocable. Stan and Betsy's ability to amend, modify, and even revoke the trust at any time, in their capacity as trustors, gives them total control over their plan. They can change successor trustees to act if they are unwilling or unable to act. They can change beneficiaries. They can change what each beneficiary receives, when, and how they receive it. They can do anything they want with their trust.

Additional Benefits of a Revocable Trust

I prefer the revocable trust because it is flexible, we avoid court-controlled estate administration out of court, and for the lifetime benefits it offers. Clients would like to keep things simple. That's not always easy. When settling a trust estate, a trust allows us to represent the trustee without going to court and facilitates the distribution of assets to the family. We can address all trust administration requirements in the confines of our office. The trust makes the transfer of the assets much simpler at that time. There is more on this in a later chapter.

What about someone who says they have very little in the way of assets? The decision about whether someone should use a trust or a will has less to do with how much they own than what you want to happen at different stages in your life. In other words, how much protection do you want?

What is appropriate for you if you have a young child, home, bank account, a company 401k, a $50,000 life insurance policy, and two pups? It depends. You still need health care documents. You need a will. If you become incapacitated, you need someone to act on your behalf on financial matters.

If your child is a minor, it would not be wise to name them as the beneficiary of an insurance policy or IRA. Again, the administration of the death benefit will require a court proceeding. The court will set up a testamentary trust and appoint someone you may not know to administer the trust and its investments for the benefit of your minor child until they reach majority age. If you name your estate as the policy's beneficiary, that also requires probate. Is that what you want?

With the revocable trust, you avoid those issues. Your revocable trust can be written to create a sub-trust for the benefit of your minor child after your death. The trust is named the primary beneficiary of your policy. All your other assets are correctly titled in the sub-trust name or connected to the sub-trust by the appropriate beneficiary designation. You appoint the successor trustee who oversees your child's estate, all without the oversight of a court.

The sub-trust holds assets for the minor child's benefit. During the term of the sub-trust, the trustee can use the income and principal for the beneficiary as you specify until the beneficiary reaches an age you set for final distribution. At that point, the trustee distributes the remaining assets to the beneficiary.

The point is, the specific estate planning tools you choose are seldom about how much money you have. Your family situation, your challenges, and your objectives are more important.

Now that we know the parties to the trust and a few of its benefits let's examine the steps required to complete the process of designing an estate plan utilizing a revocable trust in greater detail.

Designing Your Trust Plan

This is where working with an experienced estate planning attorney begins paying you a return on your investment. This is where you notice you are working with excellence. This is where free or low-cost services offered by downloadable documents off the internet or Legal Zoom reach the point of failure.

The estate planning process begins with a series of straightforward questions. What follows is certainly not a comprehensive list. It is the beginning of the design phase of your plan.

The fact that you are sitting with an experienced estate planning attorney so you can understand more about estate planning and explore your options indicates you have taken the first step toward handling your business and financial affairs responsibly.

Congratulations!

At some point, the conversation will lead to discovery about who you are and your goals. It may feel like filling out one of those lengthy forms they put in front of you on a clipboard when visiting the doctor. At this point, the process focuses on a diagnosis. Prescription comes later.

The questions will start with the basics.

- What have you done so far?
- What are your goals?
- What do you own?
- How did you acquire it?
- How is the asset titled today?
- What is the value of each asset?
- What is your net worth?
- How many children do you have?
- What is their health?
- How would you describe their financial maturity?
- Do they have children? What are their ages?
- What is the status of their marriage?
- How are you going to divide the estate?
- When will they receive the money?
- If outright, are they financially mature enough to handle it?
- Who will manage the administration of your estate?
- What happens to your estate if the surviving spouse remarries?

These questions spawn others and lead to a deeper exploration of your goals, challenges, and family situation. Other questions center around health care matters. Income and estate tax issues arise. If your situation and goals demand it, the experienced attorney will open a discussion about estate tax, asset protection, or business succession planning. It may lead to considering how to avoid losing all your assets if you or your spouse must enter a nursing home.

There will be discussions about your financial and investment planning. How are you prepared for your retirement years? When should you begin taking Social Security? Is this a good time to convert your traditional IRA to a Roth IRA? There are many others.

As the questions evolve, this is where the payoff for using an experienced attorney becomes evident. The questions become more artful. This is where the obstacles get addressed, and a pathway to completing your plan emerges. Your attorney should lead you through a discussion that often causes you to say, "I hadn't thought about that". Yet, this is not the most critical part of the conversation.

The most critical part appears when you ask a question pertinent to your situation. You might think it is a little far out. Perhaps you have a delicate family situation requiring more careful analysis and decision-making. That free, downloadable document off the internet will not work through that issue with you. No one at the other end of the Legal Zoom phone will know how to probe into the bottomless crevasses of your family situation to help you identify and address your most important concerns and questions and weave them into an appropriate plan for your family.

A few days ago, a financial advisor who refers clients to us was in my office. She said she had a married couple with a pretty complicated farm and ranch situation. The wife inherited a significant amount of farmland in another state. An S-corporation owned the farm. The farm had been in her family for three generations. There were leases to operators and producing minerals. She was asking question after question. I loved it.

Business owner clients and farm and ranch operations are in my wheelhouse. The complexities can be endless. Often, there are as many emotional issues as financial, estate, and tax issues. The point is when the right questions are asked, possibilities reveal themselves.

Decisions You Will Make

Let's reset the scene with Stan and Betsy. You recall they created a revocable trust. They appeared in the document as the trustors because they own the assets and are the ones creating the plan. They are named beneficiaries so they can continue to use the trust assets to support their lifestyle. They also name themselves trustees to ensure they can manage trust assets as they did before. As trustees, they retain decision-making authority over their assets.

Now we can center our focus. There are two significant decisions to make. First, how will your estate be managed during your lifetime if you become disabled? Second, how will the estate be distributed at your death?

Management of Your Trust Estate

It is the trustee who has management control over your trust assets. You will serve in that capacity as long as you are willing and able. If you are married, both will serve as long as either is willing and able. Then the question is, who will you select to be your successor trustee when neither of you can serve?

Your choice of a successor trustee is a critical decision. You are assigning a tremendous amount of responsibility to someone or an entity you select as your successor trustee. It is a J-O-B.

In Stan and Betsy's case, assume they create a trust. They stipulate that if one becomes incapacitated, the other has complete management power and control over the assets. If either of them becomes incapacitated, the other trustee can continue to use assets titled in the trust and the money those assets generate for the care and well-being of themselves and the incapacitated spouse.

When creating their trust, they selected a successor trustee. It can be a person or corporation who assumes management of trust assets if Stan and Betsy are both unable and unwilling to serve as trustee. It is a significant responsibility.

When does the successor trustee assume their duties? Either Stan or Betsy might have passed away, and the other might have become disabled. In that situation, the successor trustee would assume management responsibilities. Or, perhaps both Stan and Betsy have passed away. At that point, the successor trustee assumes responsibility for the management of the trust estate.

Who does it make sense to choose to assume successor trustee responsibilities? Is it a child? Is it two children jointly? Is it a third party such as an institutional trustee, a trust company, or a bank trust department? You might select a trusted advisor or relative with a deep understanding of financial affairs.

When you name someone to be a successor trustee, their responsibilities are similar to those of someone serving as the personal representative of your estate if you used a last will as the foundation of your planning. Many of the steps required of your successor trustee are the same.

That selection of your successor trustees is crucial. You want to make sure you choose someone with the experience, significant financial maturity, willingness, and time to perform the task and accept the responsibility. Said again, serving as a successor trustee is a J-O-B.

Recently, a client approached me. He had been named the successor trustee of his aunt's trust. The aunt had no living descendants. Her beneficiaries were her sister for a specific amount to be paid over ten years and her three nieces and nephews who were to receive the balance of her estate. The nieces and nephews were raising Cain because their shares were to be held in trust for their benefit for a period of time. They wanted the money NOW and were threatening litigation and generally being pains in the derriere. All my client, the successor trustee, could ask was how he could get out of the responsibility and whether we would assume the trustee role in his place.

Managing the Distribution of Your Trust

Most people wish to leave their estate to their children in equal shares. Logical questions follow. When will they receive the money? Is it an immediate distribution where they receive the money and other assets outright and free of trust? In other words, after payment of all final expenses, does the trustee write them a check or deed property over to them as soon as possible? Or, do we believe it is more prudent to stagger the distributions out to the children over a period of time?

Suppose the trust provides for an immediate distribution, after identifying all trust assets and paying all final taxes and expenses. In that case, the successor trustee can write the beneficiary a check and take the final steps to settle the estate.

If you decide an immediate distribution is not prudent, a good approach is to decide an age at which you are comfortable having the trustee write the child a check for the remaining balance and close that child's trust share. If that age is 40, are there interim ages at which you decide the trustee can make staggered distributions of trust principal?

You may choose different distribution ages or multiple ages. You might decide to hold the estate in trust for the children until they reach age 25. Or, you might choose 30 and 40 as the final distribution age. You might choose to have the trust estate held in trust for the benefit of your children during their lifetime, then pass the estate on to your grandchildren and great-grandchildren during their lifetime. Your children would receive liberal distributions of trust income and principal during their lifetime. The decision to benefit multiple generations of your family is often referred to as generational or dynasty planning.

Here is a simple example. Because their children are still relatively young, Stan and Betsy decide they do not want an immediate distribution of trust assets to their children. They also decide that by age 35, each of the children will be financially mature enough to have received the entire trust estate. They also decide partial distributions are appropriate. They decide their children will receive one-third of their trust share at 25, one-third at 30, and the final one-third at 35.

This is a good time to clarify a point about distributions. If your trust estate is set up to pay out distributions over a period, we distinguish between discretionary and mandatory distributions.

Discretionary v. Mandatory Distributions

Suppose the trust agreement provides that the money is to be held in trust until a beneficiary reaches a certain age or certain ages. The trust may stipulate that trust assets will be distributed over a certain period or that a specific percentage of the estate is to be paid out each year. Regardless, the trustee will invest the trust assets to balance both the beneficiaries' current and future security needs.

During the entirety of the trust term, in Stan and Betsy's case to age 35, the trustee is typically given the discretion to make distributions for a beneficiary's health, education, maintenance, and support. Those terms are broadly defined. For example, "education" can include expenses for K-12 and post-secondary costs. Field trips can be included. Expenses such as air and rail travel for study abroad programs can be covered. Expenses for vocational training can be covered.

In some instances, clients want to limit discretionary distributions by the trustee. Some families have children with drug or alcohol issues. They insist the child be drug-free as determined by periodic testing for a couple of years. Children may be incarcerated. Some are spendthrifts with the financial maturity normally found in first graders. You may have a child with special needs. Some are magnets for lawsuits and financial mischief.

By contrast, when designing your trust plan, you can stipulate that when a beneficiary reaches a certain age or ages, the trustee is required to make a mandatory distribution. In Stan and Betsy's case, mandatory distributions and the amount distributed would be triggered at 25, 30, and 35 years of age. Even then, if any of the conditions appearing in the previous paragraph are present, the trustee has the authority to place limitations on mandatory distributions.

This week a successor trustee decided he would exercise his rights to not make distributions to a specific beneficiary. Provisions in the trust agreement authorized him to take this step. The specific concern was the beneficiary was involved in litigation. If the beneficiary lost his case and a judgment was taken against him, he might lose it all if he had received his inheritance.

Divorce and Asset Protection for Beneficiaries

During our initial discussions with clients, we discuss a multitude of issues. You may be worried about the marital status of a child. Their marriage is, shall we say, iffy. You may not relish the idea of your child inheriting your assets, then co-mingling them with their soon-to-be ex-spouse and watching him walk out of the marriage with half of your assets dangling from his hip pocket because he could not get all of it into his wallet. Other children may be in higher-risk professions, such as a physician. Creating divorce or asset protection for your children is a very wise consideration in the design phase of your planning.

After resolving these and other decisions, you should have a plan that is a perfect fit for your family at the end of the design phase. We can always create a visual of the plan's highlights on one sheet of paper and a Roadmap of steps we will be taking with the client to complete the process.

To be clear – do not try to do this yourself. Even intelligent people like yourself fumble at the estate planning goal line. Remember, this is about protecting you and your family. Act out of wisdom and seek wisdom. Get professional help. You will be glad.

The Pour-Over Will

Clients often say, "If I use a trust for my estate plan, do I need a will?" Yes. There are numerous reasons why. If your estate plan is a wheel with a hub and spokes to support it, we think of the revocable trust as the Hub. The spokes support the plan and ensure your protection during your lifetime and at the time of your demise. The pour-over will is one of these spokes.

Before we go into those answers, the obvious questions are:

What is a pour-over will, and if I have a revocable trust, why do I need a will?

Going back to Stan and Betsy, assume they created an "I love you" will twenty years ago. It stipulated all assets went to the survivor if living and if not to their children in equal shares. Unless subsequently changed, that last will remains in effect.

Assume they decide to create a new trust. It is the Hub of your plan. They will also execute a new will that works in tandem with the trust. It serves two main purposes. First, it declares this as your last will and that you are revoking all previously executed wills and codicils (amendments). The second purpose is to update their preferences for who will be the beneficiaries of their estate. Here is more detail about how this works.

Recall our discussion about intestate succession? All states have a statutory set of rules that will direct how your assets are distributed at death if you fail to create your own estate plan. Creating your own plan will override the state's formulas. The legal instrument that overrides the state's formula is a last will and testament.

When a male creates a last will he is referred to as the "testator". For ladies, the term is "testatrix". For convenience only, I will use the terms interchangeably. Courts are rigorous about the requirements to create a legal last will. There are specific steps required. First, they want to ensure the testator has the mental capacity to create the document. Second, courts want to ensure the testatrix executed her last will of her own volition, free from coercion, duress, or undue influence from a third party. Courts look for any clues of fraud or undue influence to ensure the last will is a true and complete expression of the author's intent.

Some – not all - states recognize what is called a holographic will. This is a last will written and signed in your own hand. With a holographic will, courts will be looking for proof that the testator wrote the will, evidence that he possessed the mental capacity to write the will, and that the will contains his wish to give his estate to the beneficiaries indicated in the document.

One test of mental capacity is whether the testator knows the "natural objects of his bounty." In other words, does he know his children or beneficiaries, and does he know their names? That is a low threshold to prove capacity.

Validating a holographic will can be challenging. How do you prove the testator possessed the appropriate mental capacity if they are deceased? This is compounded by the fact that a holographic will does not require witnesses or a notary to verify the person who created the last will is the person who signed it.

By contrast, the requirements for executing a formal last will are more exacting. Not perfect, but more precise. In this instance, the last will, like the holographic will, must be executed by the testator. In addition, to be self-proving, the document must be signed by witnesses. A Notary Public will attest to the parties being who they say they are and that the witnesses saw the testatrix sign the document.

To have the best chance of creating a valid last will that will be upheld in court, the testator should have the document prepared by a qualified estate planning attorney. Before signing the last will, the attorney will ask the testator questions in front of witnesses and a notary.

- Do you understand this is your last will and testament?
- Are you 18 years of age?
- Are you of sound mind?
- What are the names of your children or beneficiaries?
- Are you executing this last will of your own volition, free of duress, undue influence or coercion from anyone?
- Have you asked X and Y to witness the signing of your last will and for Z to notarize your signature?

These questions help establish a record of the testator's intent and capacity. It also creates independent third-party corroboration of that intent and capacity. Those who witness and notarize a last will may be called into court to testify as to the testator's mental condition and declarations.

Probate offers anyone having a potential beneficial interest in the estate the opportunity to contest the provisions of the last will. There have been occasions in my practice where capacity was a possible issue. Perhaps we learned there was strife within the family, and someone was likely to challenge the will's validity during the probate process. Suppose we determine that there may be an issue with mental capacity. In that case, we might videotape the ceremony so the probate judge would have additional evidence when ruling on a challenge.

Now that we know more about a last will, we can answer the question: What is a pour-over will?

Indeed, we think of a last will as the document used to identify the beneficiaries of our estate. It is the document we use to override the state's intestate distribution provisions. It identifies:

- Who receives our estate.
- When they receive it.
- How they will receive it.
- Who manages and oversees the process.

When we create a revocable trust, it becomes the document that answers those questions. However, the trust can only control what is titled in its name. In other words, what the trust owns. How does this relate to the last will?

If Stan and Betsy created a trust a few years ago and properly followed through to ensure all titled assets were re-titled in the name of the trust. Assets such as IRAs, insurance, and annuities would be directed to their trust by creating an appropriate beneficiary designation.

What if a few years later, Stan remembers he forgot to title mineral interests he inherited from his parents into the name of the trust? What if they refinanced their residence and, as a closing requirement, the title company or lender removed the home from the trust back into their joint name? And then did not offer them the courtesy of placing the house back into the trust following the closing? When either Stan or Betsy passes away, that leaves the residence titled in one name. Remember the Rule? Correct. Probate.

This is where the pour-over will comes into play. Any asset left out of the trust and titled in one person's name would go through probate. At that point, the pour-over will controls and directs where the assets are to go.

Here is the critical point. The pour-over states that the estate's beneficiary is the revocable trust Stan and Betsy created. Even though probate is required, the asset would be given to the trust when completed. Then all assets would be in the trust and paid to Stan and Betsy's trust beneficiaries.

We can think of the pour-over will as a fail-safe document that ensures all assets end up in the name of the trust. Although we hope never to use it, the pour-over will is an essential fail-safe document. It helps ensure the overall continuity of the plan Stan and Betsy created.

The pour-over will is a vital spoke supporting the wheel of your estate plan. Other spokes play an essential role as well. We now explore how you designate someone to act on your behalf regarding financial matters if you cannot do so yourself.

The Power of Attorney for Finance

Another vital spoke to the estate planning wheel is the durable financial power of attorney. This document identifies an agent who is empowered to act on your behalf if you cannot act for yourself. Even when utilizing a trust as the centerpiece of your plan, a power of attorney to handle financial matters is an absolute.

The type of power of attorney is "durable" because the power granted to your agent to act on your behalf extends beyond your incapacity. In some states, previous law provided that when you create a power of attorney and designate someone to act on your behalf, your agent's authority is terminated upon your incapacity. That defied logic and has been remedied in virtually all states.

A power of attorney for financial transactions can be effective upon signing the document. Or, it can be structured so that it springs into effect after verifying your incapacity.

The method for determining your incapacity can be either the standard used by most practitioners, "two physicians in writing" or, state law permitting, the alternative of creating a "disability panel."

Finding two physicians to make a written declaration of incapacity can be challenging. If you have a regular treating physician, they will usually respond quickly. Securing another written opinion often takes long enough that someone's health might be at risk.

When a trust is the foundation of your estate plan, and all assets are correctly titled in the trust name or connected to the trust via a proper beneficiary designation, it is the person you designated as your trustee who has control over trust assets. It is important to remember that in the context of avoiding probate, we focus only on the asset side of your financial statement. The title to your assets are changed from your name, or joint name if married, to the trust name. We do not modify the liabilities. They remain in your name. A lender may require that your loan is set up in the name of your trust and that you sign the promissory note in your capacity as trustee. In that case, your successor trustee could act on behalf of the trust. However, that is not typical.

In most cases, the original loan and promissory note are in your personal name. If so, your trustee has no authority to renew the note if required by the bank. Suppose the note needs to be renewed or extended. Only the agent named in your power of attorney could handle that for you. If you cannot sign a tax return, only the agent named in your power of attorney has the authority to sign for you. If it is discovered one of your assets, say a bank account, is still titled in your individual name, with a well-drafted power of attorney, your agent should be able to go to the bank, present identification along with a copy of the document and transfer ownership of the bank account to the trust.

How might this work in real-time? Suppose our protagonist, Stan, is away on a fishing trip with his buddies in Chile, South America. Somewhere in Patagonia. Back home, while Stan is standing in a beautiful, clear stream fly fishing for trout, an issue that requires his attention arises. The information he submitted to renew his business line of credit was missing his signature on one of the forms. The line of credit expires today, and Stan cannot be reached. The bank would probably give Stan a good-grace extension until he returns. What if they refused, thus triggering a default on the loan?

A financial power of attorney would be vital if Stan is incapacitated and can no longer manage his business affairs. In many cases, the need for an agent to act on your behalf on a financial transaction may be more subtle yet equally important. For example, Stan may be in excellent health but just coming out of surgery. He needs someone else to handle a financial matter for him. It could be a brokerage account that requires a signature. As mentioned, Stan needs someone authorized to sign the 1040 tax return with Betsy. Or, if Stan's signature is required to close a real estate transaction and he was climbing Mt. Kilimanjaro with a team of friends from college. Or if a change is required to an IRA account or beneficiary form on a life insurance policy and he was unavailable. The possibilities and circumstances requiring a power of attorney are almost endless.

So, we ask - while Stan is on his trip, is there anyone empowered to act for him on financial matters? Is this power somehow granted to Betsy simply because they are married? Is a wife automatically given legal authority to act on their husband's behalf on financial matters? Even if someone does have the power to act for Stan, is there a limit to what they can do for Stan? Is there a time limit on the authority?

Quite often, the person selected as the successor trustee in the trust is also designated as the agent in the power of attorney. In that case, that individual may be required to wear two hats. In exercising their responsibilities on behalf of trust assets, they wear their successor trustee hat. In the case of acting for you on the individual matters we discussed, they are wearing the power of attorney agent's hat.

The financial power of attorney is a powerful spoke supporting our estate planning wheel. What about other spokes? What are those, and what is required of them to adequately support your plan?

Life Care Planning

As you saw, to protect yourself during your lifetime, you certainly need a durable power of attorney for financial purposes. The same is true regarding health care matters. On the health care side of your life, each of these documents should be in place: a power of attorney for healthcare, an Advance Directive, sometimes referred to as a living will, a Health Insurance Portability and Accountability Act ("HIPAA") release form, and perhaps a Do-Not-Resuscitate ("DNR") document.

Each state has its own version of what physical conditions must be present to activate the advance directive. In our state, the advance directive is the document that declares what treatment you want if two physicians state, in writing, you are 1) persistently unconscious, 2) terminal or 3) you are in an end-of-life condition. There is no national Uniform Living Will standard, so each state will have different conditions covered by the directive.

Sometimes you hear the advance directive referred to as the "pull the plug" document. That is an unappealing but accurate, description. Generally, the document is used very close to the time of death. Some people do not want to be intubated – kept alive on a machine - just to prolong an inevitable outcome. Most want comfort care of some kind, pain relief, and to be kept comfortable.

On the other hand, your health care power of attorney is used more frequently during your lifetime. For example, Stan falls in his bathroom at home and is rendered unconscious. He is wheeled into the hospital on a gurney and remains unable to communicate. Stan is not yet terminal, persistently unconscious, nor in an end-stage condition. In that instance, the agent Stan designated in his health care power of attorney, most likely Betsy would be acting on his behalf.

The same would apply if you have a heart attack and are temporarily unable to act for yourself. In neither of those cases, it would be too early for the Advance Directive to apply. In those cases, your health care power of attorney agent would be the person making decisions and consulting with your medical team.

You should execute a HIPAA form. The Privacy Rule protects all "individually identifiable health information" held or transmitted by a covered entity or its business associate, in any form or media, whether electronic, paper or oral. By law, medical providers cannot share details about your medical treatment without your express approval. The HIPAA document states who you approve to receive information about your medical treatment or condition. In effect, your HIPAA form trumps the Privacy Rule and allows your medical team to share information about your situation and treatment with those you designate on the form.

What about the Do Not Resuscitate document, referred to as the DNR? Some want this form executed; others do not. In most states, if you have an event at your home and call an emergency service provider, state law requires them to resuscitate, even if you possess a DNR. Once in the hospital, they will not resuscitate if you have a DNR. But here is the question. If you are in the hospital, wouldn't you want the doctors and their team to take every step possible to keep you going? At least until you reach one of those three conditions where your advance directive becomes operative? Again, everyone feels differently. It is a topic worth your time and consideration.

We also provide our clients with a Docubank card. Sometimes you are away from home, visiting grandchildren, out to dinner on a Saturday night, attending a football game at your alma mater, taking your school-age kids on a summer vacation, or just getting away for a weekend golf trip. You have an accident. They take you to the hospital. They will first ask whether you have a living will, a health care power of attorney, a HIPAA release, and a DNR.

What if all your health care documents were encrypted and stored on a secure server and immediately available to the hospital when you do not have access to your documents? Docubank provides that service. When you enter the hospital, they will find the Docubank card in your wallet or purse. When they dial the 800 number, the hospital will receive your health care documents within a few minutes.

+ My Emergency Info & Medical Directives

CALL **800-362-8226**   **DOCUBANK.COM**

Jane B. Example
Member #: **987654**   PIN: **3210**

Allergies: Penicillin, codeine, morphine
Conditions: Diabetes, asthma

Medication List on File

Contact: Jonathan Example
          Cell: 610-667-3524 *Home:* 610-667-4184 *Work:* 610-667-9726

Provided Through: **John Q. Law, Esq.**
Law & Stevenson, P.C. 610-667-3524
www.johnqlaw.com

An example of a Docubank card that you carry in your purse or wallet. In case of an emergency, this card gives a hospital immediate access to all of your healthcare documents.

The advance directive, health care power of attorney, HIPAA, and for some, a DNR provides the lifetime health care protection everyone needs. With the trust as the hub of the wheel, the pour-over will, financial power of attorney, and health care spokes in place, the wheel is complete. There is one crucial piece missing.

Activating Your Trust

This step is critical. This is where you cash your first of many estate planning dividend checks. For a trust to be "legal", it must own an asset. After the trust is designed and executed, your assets must be re-titled into the name of the trust. Why? Because the trust can only control and dispose of assets it owns.

We refer to the process of transferring ownership of your assets into the trust as "funding" the trust. This means all assets that carry a title. That includes bank accounts, CDs, stocks, bonds, mutual funds, real estate, mineral interests, and private business interests, whether held as stock in a corporation, an LLC, or partnership,

There is always an exception to the rule. Some assets are not retitled into the name of the trust. Assets such as your IRAs, 401ks, annuities, and life insurance, for example, transfer upon your death by a beneficiary designation you completed when you purchased or signed up for that asset. In most cases, assets that transfer by beneficiary designation are not subject to probate. For these assets, it is essential to modify the beneficiary designations to be consistent with the goals and objectives of your estate plan. These choices also carry important tax consequences.

Mistakes are made with beneficiary designations. If you name a primary beneficiary and they survive you, there is no issue. However, suppose the primary beneficiary predeceases you, and there is no designated beneficiary. In that case, your estate becomes the beneficiary, and you have just converted a non-probate asset to an asset requiring probate to clear title.

All of us own assets that do not have a title or deed reflecting our ownership. You may have purchased them with a Bill of Sale, written a check, or paid for them with a credit card. Those assets include your household items such as silver, china, jewelry, collections, artwork, machinery, tools, wagons, growing crops, crops in storage, and so forth. Those assets must be properly conveyed to your trust as well.

Here is the Straight Shooter's point about funding your trust. After the funding, it is business as usual. There are no new tax returns, no property tax issues, and life continues.

And again, do you remember "The Rule" about assets titled in an individual's name? They require probate, right? When your assets are titled in the trust name, how many assets are in that individual's name? The answer is zero. Thus, you avoid exposure to probate.

Maintaining Your Trust

Congratulations! You took a magnificent step to protect yourself during your lifetime and make the transfer of your assets to your beneficiaries easier to achieve. The pandemic created the opportunity and need for us to reevaluate and reconsider our planning strategies to ensure the trust our existing clients created – often many years ago - reflects their wishes. With your plan in place, there are a few points to discuss and issues that deserve your ongoing attention.

Too often. we view the process of setting up an estate plan as a "one and done" event in our lives. We want it to be a one and done deal, right? Who wants to spend their valuable time fussing over death and taxes?

Failing to maintain your estate plan is a mistake.

You change the oil in your car every few thousand miles to extend the engine's useful life. We know regular exercise, and diet discipline maintains the workability of our bodies. Likewise, you should review your estate plan every few years. We encourage our clients to review their plan every three years, at a minimum.

Keep in mind that your life changes, the law changes, and our recommendations change. Circumstances and family relationships are as unpredictable as the weather. Family members move away, pass away, or get in the way. Today's healthy child develops a disability over the weekend. Today's financially skilled child is bankrupt tomorrow. Today's happily married child is in a marriage crumbling faster than your breaking heart. Eager beaver legislators pass laws that unwitting presidents and governors sign without regard to what steps you took a few years ago or the unintended consequences they often create. Our study, experience, and knowledge from working with thousands of families create a common sense approach that influences and informs our recommendations.

You should re-evaluate your estate plan every two or three years. Sooner, if one of the points in the previous paragraph becomes your reality. When you return to the attorney who helped craft your plan design, have them take you through the process just as they did before. It should feel like your annual physical exam. Well, not exactly like that, but you get the point. You want to review the vital decisions – your estate planning cholesterol level, your estate planning blood pressure, and your estate planning inflammation level. Said more directly, how are your assets titled, who manages assets for you if you are incapacitated or die, and who receives your money?

Financial Agents

Review who you selected to serve and act on your behalf. Are the successor trustees you designated to manage and distribute your trust estate, the designated agents holding your financial and healthcare powers of attorney, or the guardians for minor children still the best choice? Are they available, willing, and able? Are the backup successor trustees the appropriate parties to manage and oversee the trust estate stribution process? Given the current environment, having your ealth care agents in close proximity might make a difference.

Your financial power attorney documents should be reviewed regularly in this environment dominated by a pandemic and other uncertainties. For example, should your agent be given absolute authority to make gifts on your behalf, or should your agent's gifting authority be limited to de minimis amounts?

It would also be appropriate to review the provisions about delegating to your agents' powers to help accomplish your tax planning goals. Provisions should include the authority to enter other types of estate planning transactions, exercise disclaimer planning, and the power to modify beneficiary designations or ownership of non-probate property such as your IRAs, life insurance, and annuities.

> Remember, your successor trustee has a fiduciary obligation to your beneficiaries and that includes preserving the value of your trust estate.

You would undoubtedly want to grant your agent the authority to access your digital assets, including email accounts, digital currencies, and online account credentials. Many of these powers are not explicitly enumerated in the more general grants of authority contained in a traditional financial power of attorney. For entrepreneurial clients granting your agent specific authority to handle tax matters, company computer systems, online banking, and payroll and HR benefits are essential.

As I mentioned before, we have also experienced feedback from clients that banks may refuse to allow your agent to act on your behalf

if the power of attorney document is more than five years old. Updat
your power of attorney document from time to time.

Health Care Agents

Another document that requires a regular review is your advance
health care directive, often referred to as a living will. Most of our
clients have decided that they do not want to be kept alive on a machine.
In other words, no intubation. In our state, if two physicians say you
are terminal, persistently unconscious, or are experiencing what the
physicians say is an end-stage condition, you can state whether or not
you wish to be kept alive on a machine.

Covid – 19 changed this dynamic somewhat. Some Covid - 19
patients who require ventilation have often plunged into a coma; others
have received treatment that included a medically induced coma. It may
not be clear how your Do – Not – Resuscitate (DNR) order applies to a
Covid - 19 patient who rapidly falls into a coma.

Because of the novelty of Covid – 19 treatments, everyone should
carefully review their current advance health care directives with their
physician and legal counsel and determine whether changes might more
fully reflect their wishes. While not a very pleasant family discussion,
sharing your healthcare wishes with your loved ones and anyone else
who may be your designated healthcare agents would be wise. They
deserve to know your expectations about how you want them to handle
their respective roles and duties.

Review Your Plan Design

Think of this like you did during the initial design phase of creating your plan. Review these issues:

- Who receives your estate, and how and when the assets will be distributed to your beneficiaries. Are your beneficiaries stated correctly? Is the share each beneficiary receives stated accurately? Are the ages each beneficiary receives all or a portion of their trust share correctly stated? If a beneficiary pre-deceases you, does that beneficiary's share go to your intended contingent beneficiaries?
- Who did you select to serve as your successor trustee. Are your original selections still appropriate?
- What actions will your trustee be required to take upon your incapacity? Upon your death? There is a process involved here. The first steps will include terminating social security payments, payment of final expenses, debts, and taxes from your trust estate.
- Distributions of your non-titled personal property we referred to as your "stuff." These distributions come in a variety of layers. Some of our stuff carries significant value, be it financial or emotional. Did you create a Memorandum of Personal Property and identify a particular person you want to receive specific non-titled assets? Is the list still accurate? Is the list included with your estate planning documents so your successor trustee will easily find it? If there is no list, did you tag or label individual items and who receives them, or create a lottery process that creates an equitable process?
- Consider any specific gifts you made to charities, religious organizations, or individuals. Are those still appropriate

recipients? Are there new beneficiaries? Are the assets you wish to bequest correctly identified? Are the amounts? Are there any changes you wish to make?

Suppose you have specified a specific amount of money to be paid to a beneficiary – charitable or individual – and experienced a decline in the value of your estate. In that case, it may be a good time to re-evaluate the amounts of those bequests. If lifetime gifts of assets with a significant value have been made to one beneficiary, it might be time to adjust the formula for what other beneficiaries receive. Failure to address these issues increases the odds of estate litigation if your objective is to leave everything to your children in equal shares.

Also, review any unique directions you gave your successor trustee regarding permitted distributions. For example, if assets are held in trust for a beneficiary until they reach 30, what costs and expenses can be covered by a discretionary distribution? Health? Yes. Education? Certainly. Maintenance or support? Probably. Down payment on a residence? Perhaps? Start a new business? Your trustee will need to know more. A new Ferrari? No.

Asset Review

Your review should include an updated asset list that includes current values and how the asset is titled. When operating and maintaining your trust estate, it is paramount all assets be properly titled in the trust name or connected to your trust via the proper beneficiary designation.

Recall, some assets are not titled in the trust name – retirement accounts, annuities, and most life insurance policies. The proper beneficiary designation is important. Failure to get this right can have financial consequences. Be sure you have designated both a primary and secondary beneficiary. Do not leave either option blank for it could result in your estate becoming a beneficiary, thus converting a non-probate transfer to one requiring probate.

Recent Developments

Because of the pandemic, many courts across the country suspended non-essential functions. As I mentioned before, probates take too long anyway. The suspensions have eased somewhat, but the limited access to court proceedings has exacerbated the difficult process of settling and distributing an estate through probate. The already burdened system is backlogged even more. That means more frozen accounts, more frustration, more inconvenience, more expense, and more delays. Now more than ever, the benefit of utilizing a revocable living trust to bypass the quagmire of court control becomes clear.

If a pandemic does not get your attention about the importance of creating an estate plan, nothing will. Experiencing the mortality of friends and loved ones brings the importance of proper planning front and center, up close and personal. The global Covid-19 pandemic reminds us about the uncertainty of life and how quickly severe illness and death can befall us. The following points are as relevant for those contemplating a plan as they are for those who currently have a plan in place.

Awareness of the consequences of the pandemic should cause us to wonder about our preparedness. Take health care issues, for example. If our health deteriorates to the point where our doctors say we are terminal, have an end-stage condition, or tell our family our persistent unconscious state is permanent, have we declared our preference about "pulling the plug"? In those instances, do we want to be kept alive on a machine?

Have we declared our desire, or did we pass that responsibility onto another person, perhaps even a child? Is that the right thing to do? Who will pay our bills if we go through a long illness requiring an extended period of recuperation? What about minor children? Who would be responsible for their financial security and care in the event of our death or incapacity?

Comprehensive plans address these and other questions. Yet the pandemic adds a new dimension to both lifecare and death planning. It focuses on the need to create a relevant, comprehensive, and effective plan. It also reminds us that if we have a plan in place, we must review it frequently to ensure it will perform in this new post-Covid-19 environment.

Now is also an excellent time to keep all of your estate planning documents close at hand and keep your loved ones and fiduciaries apprised of their location.

The Changing Situation

Change is ever-present and often painful. The Covid virus and its variants continue to run their course. We will likely have more variants until their impact and vaccinations diminish and we reach herd immunity. Lives have been lost and fear occupies a greater portion of our conscious mind than we would like. Jobs, careers, and businesses have been disrupted or destroyed. Volatile markets give us pause about our financial security. Travel restrictions and lockdowns kept us tethered to our homes. Just as things opened up, inflation appeared and cut our standard of living.

We just hope we are not like the infant elephant whose leg is chained to a stake and, upon reaching adulthood never tries to escape. Early on, we were told to minimize our risk of encountering this airborne virus by social distancing at least six feet, exercising caution about being around large groups, masking up, frequently washing our hands, and getting vaccinated.

If not, here is what can happen.

Interest rates have been historically low for the past decade or longer. Virtually all homeowners have found it wise to refinance their homes. Assume you have an estate plan in place and that you have chosen a revocable trust as the foundation of your plan. You have activated your trust plan by properly retitling assets into your trust's name and properly linking assets that transfer by beneficiary designations to your trust. Now you decide it makes economic sense to refinance your home.

Typically, the lender will require you to create a new deed transferring ownership of your residence from the trust back into your individual or joint name with your spouse if you are married. The loan closes, and the lender does not offer to return your residence to the trust's name. You forget the importance of this step. You fail to review your plan in detail with your attorney. Now you have created a situation that might require probate. The value of your plan has diminished due to neglect.

It also happens when you purchase an annuity, life insurance policy, set up a new IRA, acquire a car, or acquire real estate, either a new residence or investment property. Every time we have a client education event or send out a newsletter, we always start by asking:

"Any time you purchase an asset, you take title to it in what name?"

"When you purchase an asset that requires a primary and contingent beneficiary designation, what name should be included?"

Our clients are pretty good. They know the questions are coming and like a chorus in harmony, they shout out...

"In the name of the trust!"

There are other reasons for maintaining your estate plan.

A couple of years ago, we received a call from a frustrated gentleman who had gone to the bank to conduct some business for his ailing mother. His mother was a client. We set up her plan about ten years earlier. At the bank, the son presented his mother's power of attorney naming him as her primary agent, along with his identification.

The bank refused his request.

The power of attorney document was excellent if I do say so myself. What was the basis of the bank's refusal to allow him to conduct business on behalf of his mother?

The document was more than five years old.

What?

The bank had established a new internal rule that they would not honor a power of attorney document over five years old.

I shared this story during one of our regular client education events a few weeks later. People were aghast. Disbelief fell on the crowd like a fast-approaching storm.

"How can they do that?"

"What gives them the right to do that?"

When the storm passed, another client raised his hand. I acknowledged him. He shared that he had gone to a large regional bank and presented a power of attorney to act on behalf of his father. The bank refused because the document was more than one year old. Now the audience was agitated. The storm started to develop a funnel. I was just hoping it would not touch down and cause physical damage.

Be clear, I am not saying this is a universal concern. The proper label at this point is that these experiences are anecdotal. Yet we should not ignore the trends and risks of not keeping our plan and the documents that comprise our plan up to date. This especially applies to health care documents.

At all times, like the Boy Scout motto I learned at a young age – Be Prepared.

Responsibilities of Your
Successor Trustee

There is great satisfaction helping families create their estate plan. Our goal is that our family of clients have abundance, great relationships, and peace of mind during their lifetime. Having an estate and financial plan in place directly addresses two of those goals and certainly contributes to achieving the third.

Designing and activating the plan is the fun part. Implementing it after losing a client is less so.

Because of our regular communications with clients, they know to call us if a spouse or parent has a health issue, is about to enter a nursing home, or upon their passing. Many of them have informed their children that we are the first call.

Nearly all of them have utilized a revocable trust as the foundation of their estate plan. There are steps to be taken at the first and second death or upon a pending disability issue. We take these steps to ensure your plan works as designed and as you intended.

Who Do I Choose?

Most people tread too lightly when choosing who will oversee the distribution of their estate. We must be sure the decision is based on capability, not fear. We should not select our successor trustee because someone might be angry at us for our choice. We should choose our successor trustee because we trust them, their ability, and willingness to serve.

Suppose the distribution of our estate is conducted through a probate according to the terms of your last will. The person overseeing the administration and distribution of your estate is referred to as the personal representative. They used to be labeled the executor or executrix.

If you have created a trust, your successor trustee handles the administration and distribution of your trust estate. The duties and responsibilities of administering a probate estate and trust estate are very similar, except the trust estate does not require probate or court supervision.

This is an important point. A successor trustee has a fiduciary duty to the beneficiaries. That includes current and possible future beneficiaries. What does it mean to have a fiduciary duty to beneficiaries of a trust?

There are three requirements to satisfy the fiduciary duties of a trustee: a duty of loyalty, a duty of care, and the duty of full disclosure.

To satisfy the duty of loyalty, the trustee must manage the trust in a way that is in the best interest of the beneficiaries. That means all beneficiaries. A trustee cannot act in their own interests or the interests of other specific individuals at the expense of the beneficiaries. All actions that trigger a conflict of interest could be considered a breach of loyalty and will likely be considered illegal.

For example, a conflict of interest could arise if the trustee holds a bias towards one of the beneficiaries, if personal assets are commingled with the assets in the trust, or if trust assets are purchased at a price below fair market value for the trustee's own benefit. If there is a biased relationship with a specific beneficiary, the trustee might not be able to make decisions that are in the best interest of all beneficiaries. The duty of loyalty also prohibits "self-dealing." This can occur when a trustee uses assets in the trust for personal reasons.

Suppose the trustee is also a beneficiary of the estate. What if the trustee uses trust assets to upgrade or repair real estate the trustee will receive as part of her share of the estate? What if the trustee leverages their position for personal price benefits from a vendor that does business with the trust during the administration phase? This list of potential violations of a trustee's fiduciary duty due to a breach of loyalty can be quite long.

The duty of care means the trustee must avoid actions that could harm the beneficiaries – individually or collectively. A trustee must act as any other "reasonably" prudent person would when managing a trust. It is possible that if a trustee is skilled in an area relating to the management of the trust, they will be held to a higher standard of care when it comes to making decisions in those areas on behalf of the trust.

The final component of a trustee's fiduciary duty centers on the duty of full disclosure to all beneficiaries. This can become an issue if a trustee refuses to share a copy of the trust with a beneficiary, fails to notify beneficiaries of information relevant to the performance of trust assets, or does not share information about litigation or other legal matters. American Bar Association (ABA) standards require a "full disclosure of material facts" and stipulate the trustee is obligated to "render clear and accurate accounts of the administration of the trust."

Here are examples of actions and behaviors that would violate a trustee's fiduciary obligations:

- Exerting undue influence or pressure.
- Taking selfish advantage.
- "Self-Dealing" with the person with whom they are in a fiduciary relationship in such a way that it benefits the fiduciary or prejudices the person to whom a fiduciary duty is owed.

There can be severe penalties for trustees who fail to fulfill their fiduciary responsibilities. A "breach of fiduciary duties" may result in civil or even criminal penalties.

With these duties as a backdrop, it becomes clear that when you designate someone to serve as your successor trustee, you give them a J-O-B. This job requires their time, effort, and assumption of legal responsibility.

Selecting Your Successor Trustee

To restate what I said earlier: Your choice should be based on your level of trust with the candidate, their capability, and their willingness to accept the responsibility.

Through the years, I have opened my mind to new possibilities on this point. It's not so much a change of opinion about the requirements mentioned above. Those are sacrosanct. It simply reflects how my years of experience have shaped my feelings about the available options. In the beginning, I wanted to follow the Dacey formula by selecting a family member – typically one of the children – to assume those responsibilities.

When clients are leaning toward selecting a child as their successor trustee, I ask more detailed questions. I probe more deeply into the relationship between the proposed trustee and siblings. If the relationship is contentious, even iffy, that might suggest an independent trust. Now I understand that if the relationship is solid, that too might suggest an independent trustee. Why put great relationships at risk by naming one child to serve?

Children often have a difficult time sorting through the meaning of your selection. They may conclude that not selecting them diminishes the perceived love relationship you had with them. While love between and among family members is essential, it should not be a factor in choosing your successor trustee. Today, I am more prone to suggest clients consider an independent successor trustee to administer the trust administration and distribution of assets. Then the children have a common enemy.

Some people express concern about the expense of choosing an independent successor trustee. Most trust plans provide that whoever you choose to serve is entitled to reasonable compensation. That is the case if you select a family member or an independent trustee. I always ask: During the delicate time of wrapping up your estate, what is it worth to preserve long-term family harmony? The cost of family disputes and breakups is very, very high.

Let's not forget that the person you select as a successor trustee, personal representative, attorney-in-fact, or agent has a fiduciary obligation to you in the event of your lifetime incapacity and to your estate and its beneficiaries at your death.

In summary, when serving as a successor trustee or personal representative, the person or entity you selected must protect assets titled in the name of the trust. They must prudently invest assets unless all beneficiaries grant a specific waiver. They must provide a regular accounting to beneficiaries outlining the use of trust funds. And, they must disclose their actions to all beneficiaries and act prudently and responsibly to benefit all beneficiaries. They must always be objective and fair with the beneficiaries.

Duties of a Successor Trustee During Incapacity

Let's put these principles into action.

Assume Stan has a stroke. His condition deteriorates to a point where he can no longer conduct business for himself or manage his affairs as a co-trustee with Betsy.

The first call would be to the estate planning attorney who helped create their plan. The trust document should contain provisions addressing two critical issues: How is Stan's incapacity determined? Who is authorized to act on his behalf?

Many trusts provide that for a successor trustee to assume their duties, two physicians must issue a written opinion that Stan can no longer manage his affairs and is therefore incapacitated. When both spouses are living, this is not an issue. The trust provides that Betsy will continue to serve as sole trustee if Stan is incapacitated. She can use trust assets for her lifetime and for the care and well-being of Stan. This is another advantage of using a trust for your estate planning. But what happens if Stan passes away, and at a later point, Betsy has health issues?

Assume Stan and Betsy followed our suggestion and created a Disability Panel to decide when someone is incapacitated. The panel might consist of each spouse, if living, the children – Susan and John, and their primary physician. They decided decisions are to be made by majority vote rather than unanimous consent. With the Disability Panel, family members, perhaps aided by the treating physician, could avoid securing the written opinion of two physicians and establish incapacity by their vote. If the panel determined Betsy was incapacitated, it would trigger the powers provided in their trust, and the successor trustee would assume their responsibilities. Again, the trust provides that the successor trustee is to use trust assets for the care of Betsy during her lifetime.

If Stan and Betsy had chosen to use a last will as the foundation of their plan, or if they had no plan, a court-supervised living probate (guardianship or conservatorship) would likely be required. With a trust, provisions regarding care and how trust assets are used during incapacity are activated without court approval

Let's return to the example of what happens if Betsy becomes incapacitated following Stan's demise. The same principles apply, except the successor trustee will have more actions to take. Stan and Betsy designated Susan as their successor trustee and named her the successor agent in their power of attorney documents. Now that Betsy is incapacitated – as determined by the Disability Panel – what are Susan's responsibilities?

The estate planning attorney will work with Susan and help her become familiar with the provisions in the trust and how to follow those instructions set forth by Stan and Betsy.

To satisfy her fiduciary responsibilities, Susan will become familiar with Betsy's health care options and financial affairs. She will need to present proper documentation to financial institutions to sign checks to pay Betsy's bills. Notifications of Susan's elevation to the successor trustee role are sent to financial institutions, including those holding IRAs, 401ks, annuities, and life insurance.

There may be specific directives Stan and Betsy have outlined regarding their care. Susan will review the provisions of Betsy's Advance Directive (Living Will) regarding Betsy's end-of-life decisions, her health care power of attorney, and her HIPAA instructions about who may receive information about her medical condition and treatments.

If Stan and Betsy do not have long-term health care insurance to cover most if not all of those costs, the successor trustee should also visit with an experienced elder law attorney. That will help Susan clarify the estate's exposure to long-term health care expenses and possible strategies to ensure Betsy's estate avoids going broke from possible nursing care expenses.

The Straight Shooter's Guide To Estate Planning

In the chapter Settling Your Trust Estate, we will provide more detail about actions taken following the death of Stan and Betsy.

Some of you may be thinking, Larry, when will you talk about estate taxes? That's next.

What About Estate Tax?

Current law allows each of us to transfer our assets to people we choose, either during our lifetime or following our death. When we transfer assets to our spouse, there is no limit or restriction on the amount transferred. Transfers to others have limitations. A federal estate tax is due if we make transfers of assets during our lifetime or at death that exceed those limits. Some states have a separate inheritance or estate tax that impose taxes if transfers exceed a stipulated amount.

The amount that we can transfer to others during our lifetime is called the estate tax "exclusion." No estate tax is due if cumulative lifetime and death transfers do not exceed the exclusion amount. The exclusion amount has been modified a number of times. When my father died, the exclusion was $250,000. As of this writing, it exceeds $12 million. On January 1, 2026, the exclusion reverts to $5 million, adjusted for inflation.

The law also gives us a perk. We can make annual gifts up to a specified amount without using our lifetime exclusion. Today, that amount is $16,000. And, we can make annual gifts up to that amount to an unlimited number of people. Gifts for medical or educational purposes can exceed the annual gift exclusion.

Next, we begin valuing assets in the estate to determine our exposure to estate tax. There should never be any estate tax due at the first death unless circumstances dictate paying some tax now would benefit the overall goals of our clients and their families. We know the trust contains fail-safe language that they will be able to fully utilize both estate tax exclusions up to the amount available to them at the time of their demise.

We also determined Stan and Betsy made no taxable gifts during their lifetime that could be added back into their current net worth for determining estate tax liability. We want to take the necessary steps to protect Stan's entire estate tax exclusion.

At this point, we have two goals. Pay no estate tax at the first death and minimize, if not entirely avoid, paying estate tax at the second death.

Here is an example of effective estate tax planning.

Estate Tax Planning After the First Death

Assume Stan and Betsy create a joint revocable trust. When the trust is made, there is a stipulation that a certain percentage of the assets will be considered Stan's property, and a certain percentage will be regarded as Betsy's property. The split is usually, but not always, 50-50 for each spouse.

No Anticipated Estate Tax Exposure

If we determine that there is no estate tax exposure because the exclusions are so high relative to the estate's value, there may not be any steps taken to protect Stan's exclusion. Betsy will continue operating the trust as they did when Stan lived. The entire value of the assets will be included in Betsy's estate.

However, if her exclusion is less than the value of the estate, there will be an estate tax obligation. Do we want to take that risk? What if the law changes? What if the value of Stan and Betsy's assets increase, and we must preserve both exclusions to shelter the estate from estate taxes?

Possible Estate Tax Liability

What follows is a description of actions taken to protect Stan's estate tax exclusion upon his death. You never want to waste an estate tax exclusion. That's how families pay more in estate tax than they are legally required to pay. We always try to structure the trust to make protecting an estate tax exclusion optional and not mandatory.

Upon Stan's death, Stan's 50% share of the trust estate would be split off and retitled into a Family Trust, sometimes referred to as a Credit Shelter Trust or Bypass Trust. We take this action for two reasons: first, to preserve Stan's estate tax exclusion, and second to defer any potential estate tax liability to the time of the second death.

The 50% of the assets representing Betsy's share of the trust estate will continue to be held in the name of their joint trust. Assets held in the Family Trust will never be exposed to estate tax liability again.

Because of that, we seek to preserve the value of the Family Trust and let it grow as much as possible during Betsy's lifetime. Terms of the Family Trust cannot be revoked or amended.

Betsy would continue serving as the sole trustee of the Family Trust and have management control over trust assets. As its sole beneficiary, the Family Trust assets remain available to Betsy for her care and well-being during her lifetime. Betsy could take income and principal distributions from the trust for her health, education, maintenance, and support. Those words are significant in the context of estate tax planning. They are referred to in the IRC as "ascertainable standards" and are used to ensure Stan's assets are not included in Betsy's estate at her death.

Betsy will also remain the sole trustee and beneficiary of the original joint trust. Betsy's portion of the joint trust will continue to be revocable, meaning she retains total control over that portion of the trust. There are no restrictions on Betsy's use of her 50% share remaining in the joint trust. Combining the benefits from both the Family Trust and the original joint trust, Betsy would still have access to the entire value of the estate.

Portability

Under current law, if a decedent's estate does not exceed the current estate tax exclusion amount, there is no requirement to file a Form 706 U.S. Federal Estate Tax Return. As insurance against a change in the law or increase in the value of assets remaining in Betsy's estate, are there steps we can take to preserve Stan's exclusion? Yes.

We can utilize a "portability" strategy that allows Stan's executor to transfer, or "port," Stan's unused exclusion to Betsy's exclusion she has remaining at the time of her death. Portability has been part of federal estate tax law since 2011. A Revenue Procedure issued in 2017 allows an executor up to two years to file a 706 Estate Tax return and elect portability, provided that no estate tax return is otherwise due at the first death.

Here is a simple illustration. Assume:

- The value of Stan and Betsy's estate is $4 million;
- Stan's share of the estate is 50%, or $2 million;
- The estate tax exclusion at Stan's death is $3 million per person;
- The value of the estate is $6 million at the time of Betsy's death.

At first glance, you would think there is no estate tax exposure. Stan and Betsy have a total exclusion of $6 million to protect them from paying estate tax on their $6 million estate at Betsy's death. There is a catch.

The estate tax exclusion is a "use it or lose it" proposition. If we do not take steps to preserve Stan's exclusion at the time of his death, we lose the opportunity to add it to Betsy's exclusion upon her death. If we lose Stan's exclusion, Betsy would only have her $3 million exclusion to shelter the $6 million estate. The estate would pay approximately $1.2 million in estate tax. Only because they failed to protect Stan's exclusion within two years following his death are they now paying estate tax. These are taxes they were not legally obligated to pay but for their failure to protect Stan's exclusion. In tennis, they call this an unforced error.

There is little worse than seeing a family pay taxes to the federal government they could have legally avoided. By filing a 706 Estate Tax return at Stan's death and claiming $2 million of his exclusion based on his share of the estate, we would then elect to port any unused amount over to Betsy's exclusion. Her estate would then have $4 million to shelter the remaining value of the estate, and assuming values remained steady, there would be no estate tax due at her death.

Suppose the value of Stan's 50% share of the estate exceeds the exclusion available at his death. Remember, any amount given to a spouse is not subject to the estate tax exclusion limit. In that case, the trust should provide a mechanism so that the amount exceeding the exclusion is given to Betsy for use during her lifetime, perhaps outright, in a marital trust or a trust giving her the power to appoint trust assets to anyone she chooses. This will also defer any estate tax to the second death.

Those are among the actions taken after the first spouse's death if we determine both estate tax exclusions must be preserved to avoid paying estate tax at the second death.

After Stan's death, we will also review all beneficiary designations on annuities, IRA plans, life insurance - any asset that will transfer according to a beneficiary designation. Those assets are distributed to a designated beneficiary. These assets are included in the estate tax discussion because they are included in the estate of their deceased owner.

After both Stan and Betsy's passing, we have entered the trust administration phase. Now we turn to a discussion about settling the trust estate.

Settling The Trust Estate

Following the death of Stan and Betsy, the person or entity they designated as their successor trustee assumes management of the trust estate. In the previous chapter, we discussed the estate tax issue. Now we focus on the administrative steps to be taken.

Administrative Actions After the First Death

Assume Stan passes away first. Betsy calls the office to set an appointment. When we meet with a surviving spouse or family following a death, we first collect and review all documents to understand the plan and determine what the remaining trustee or successor trustee needs to take custody of the assets and exercise their responsibilities.

We prepare a checklist of actions Betsy takes in her role as the sole trustee. We discuss those steps with her. She retains us to prepare appropriate documents. Her assignment is to prepare an updated list of their assets. We advise her on how to determine their value at the date of Stan's death.

While Betsy is updating their financial statement, our actions include thoroughly reviewing their plan documents. They may have amended their trust, perhaps restated it in its entirety to reflect changes in their lives or changes in the law. We must understand the plan design, who has authority to act on behalf of the trust, and how assets are to be administered during Betsy's remaining lifetime.

When Betsy has completed updating their financial statement, we meet again. We review the current asset list and begin developing ideas relating to estate tax. We want to know if all the assets are titled in the name of the trust. We are looking for assets that might require probate and hope to find none.

We review beneficiary designations to determine who receives proceeds from those accounts. This is particularly important for IRAs because if Betsy is the beneficiary, she can roll over Stan's IRA into her own. Or, if Stan was receiving Required Minimum Distributions, Betsy may continue to receive what Stan was receiving. The questions continue.

Did Stan make any written instructions or bequests directing the Trustee to give non-titled personal items – rings, watches, collectibles – to specific beneficiaries upon his death? Did the trust indicate there were bequests of titled assets to be given to particular beneficiaries?

We swing back to the estate tax discussion. Do we need to establish the date of death value of trust assets? Yes. We need to compare the value of trust assets and the current estate tax exclusion. Remember, both Stan and Betsy are entitled to an estate tax exclusion. If we need to use Stan's exclusions to minimize or eliminate estate taxes, we will create and fund what our trust agreement calls a Family Trust. We will transfer ownership of Stan's share of trust assets into the Family Trust and file a Form 706 U.S. Estate Tax return with the IRS. Depending on the value of assets transferred into the Family Trust, the return will either claim Stan's total exclusion or preserve the unused portion of his exclusion by porting it over to Betsy's remaining exclusion. The trust agreement may state that forming the Family Trust is mandatory or optional depending on the need to preserve Stan's exclusion.

Valuing assets and creating the Family Trust also establishes a new tax basis for those assets. That will minimize capital gains taxes if and when assets in the Family Trust are sold. I will say more about this later.

We will take steps to notify beneficiaries, identify and pay legitimate creditors, taxes and final expenses. We will complete the distribution of the specific bequests in the trust or by a written memorandum to the designated beneficiaries. We ensure Betsy remains in control of all trust assets as trustee and sole beneficiary of the original trust and Family Trust, if created.

Actions After the Second Death

In our example, Stan and Betsy designated their daughter, Susan, as their successor trustee and personal representative if a probate is required. When meeting with Susan, we work with her to take several actions. As we did following Stan's passing, we review all documents to ensure we understood the plan and made note of any steps required to complete the distribution of the trust assets to beneficiaries.

We create documents that show financial vendors and others that Susan is the successor trustee and has the authority to act on behalf of the trust. This allows her to get her name on accounts as successor trustee and quickly take custody of the assets. Notifications are sent to beneficiaries and creditors. Susan will pay any debts, taxes, and final expenses.

Again, we take the same steps to establish the date of death value of the remaining assets in the estate. We do this to determine if we have an estate tax liability. Determining the date of death value is also critical in helping beneficiaries minimize tax liability if they decide to liquidate an asset. I mentioned this earlier. Here are more details on what is called stepping-up the tax basis of an appreciated asset.

The Step-Up Rule

The step-up rule allows beneficiaries who inherit assets to adjust the asset's tax cost of the original owner to the fair market value at the deceased's date of death. For example, suppose Stan purchased a rental property 15 years ago for $100,000. Due to depreciation and repairs, his tax basis (or the adjusted cost) for determining what capital gains tax he would pay if he sold the property is $50,000. If Stan sells the property for $150,000, he pays capital gains on $100,000.

When heirs inherit that property, the step-up rule allows them to adjust the tax basis of the property to $150,000, the fair market value established at the time of death. Why is that important?

Because all previous appreciation that might have triggered a capital gains tax if Stan sold the asset now vanishes. When the heirs sell the asset, they pay capital gains on the difference between the sales price and the fair market value at the time of Stan's death, not the difference between the sales price and Stan's tax basis. This is a significant step in income tax planning when settling an estate.

At Betsy's death, we go through many of the same steps for her estate that we did upon Stan's death. We terminate Social Security payments, order death certificates, and create an accounting system to track all trust income and expenses. We secure a taxpayer identification number for the trust estate. We begin identifying assets. We identify and pay legitimate creditors, if any, and balances due.

Again, we also begin the process of valuing assets. As before, we take this step to establish a new tax basis for appreciated assets. As I described earlier, those are assets worth more at the date of death than their purchase value or adjusted tax basis. Based on current law, heirs would only pay tax on the amount of appreciation in value that exceeds the fair market value of the assets established at the time of Betsy's death.

On the estate tax side, we determine if we have a potential tax liability and, if so, whether we have liquid assets to pay the IRS. We see that appropriate tax returns are filed on or before the following April 15th. That would include Betsy's final 1040 and a 1041 Fiduciary return for income that is recognized between the date of Betsy's death and the final estate distribution.

Simultaneously, we are reviewing Stan and Betsy's trust documents to see what provisions were made for their beneficiaries. In this case, the beneficiaries are Stan and Betsy's two children. Copies of the trust documents are sent to each beneficiary.

Once those steps are completed and all the formalities are taken care of, including paying final expenses, filing final tax returns, paying the IRS, and reporting to the beneficiaries, assets can be distributed to the beneficiaries according to the terms of the trust.

We try to settle our trust administration cases as rapidly as possible. That's our target. It does not happen all the time. What slows down the settlement process?

There may be assets that have unique challenges and require more time. Resolving partnership and business-related issues can be more complicated for business owners or farm and ranch operators.

Delays can occur with more complicated assets like real estate, especially the family home. The children may decide they will not list and sell the house until they have an estate sale. They have created an artificial delay out of a preference. Rather than immediately deed the property to them individually, they may hold the property in trust until the house sells. That is one example of a decision the successor trustee and heirs might make that creates a longer trust administration process.

Regardless, even if it takes longer, your successor trustee is in total control when settling your estate through a trust administration rather than probate. They will not be required to endure the time, expense, publicity, and possibility of multiple probates to complete their duties of settling the estate.

Distributing Your Stuff

Losing a parent is one of the most stressful experiences we have in our life. In the context of settling an estate, it has the potential to disrupt family harmony. One trigger point – one that might seem surprising but upon thought is not – is the possible disagreement over the distribution of what I called your "stuff." Dividing your personal property between and among your heirs is one of those tender spots that can be draining and overwhelming for your legal representative and beneficiaries.

Most estate planning documents treat the distribution of personal property generically. The language might stipulate that your legal representative is to "divide my personal property consisting of non-titled assets equally among my children.". Many of us minimize the impact of this nonspecific instruction and ignore the potential conflict that might be created over a set of china, handwritten notes, a family heirloom, or a piece of art. Keeping with my analogy, it can create a compound fracture out of an otherwise healthy limb.

David MacMahan spoke of these distributions in a recent article[6] when he recounted the quote of a woman taken from *Who Gets Grandma's Yellow Pie Plate* written by Marlene Stum: "My mother's funeral was a piece of cake compared to clearing out the house and closing the door." When you couple the often-sensitive nature of these

---

[6] Trusts and Estates magazine, September 2020.

distributions and the tightrope the legal representative must walk in determining who gets what and what is to be sold or donated, you begin to understand the problem.

In the *New York Times,* Paul Sullivan published an article[7] entitled, "When Dividing Assets, the Little Things Matter." Estate planning attorney, John A. Warnick, was quoted as saying:

"I asked parents to think just for a second what it would be like on Christmas morning if your children ran downstairs. There were all these presents, bright and shiny, big and small, but with no name tags on them. Can you imagine the free-for-all that would ensue?"

This potential threat to family relationships exists without regard to the heirs' net worth or the estate's value. If there is no clarity about your intention, or if there is no process identified, it can ignite an argument if someone asserts that on her deathbed, mom told her she could have her rings and jewelry. It is a fertile field where otherwise dormant childhood rivalries and jealousies may resurface.

We should be alert when any of the personal property items carry significantly more value than others. It may be important to consider an independent valuation of that particular item. If one person is to receive a disproportionately more valuable piece of art, should that excess value be offset against their distribution of the balance of the trust estate?

Should you give or promise to give certain items to your heirs during your lifetime? Doing so allows the beneficiary to enjoy the gift immediately. It enables you to explain to the recipient and other

---

[7] "When Dividing Assets, Little Things Matter", Paul Sullivan, New York Times, April 15, 2016.

beneficiaries why the gift was made to a specific individual. If the gift is quite valuable, you may want to offset that value when distributing the balance of your estate. That is accomplished by treating the gift as an advancement against the recipient's overall estate share.

Another consideration is deciding what process to use to divide personal property. One of our clients divided her personal property into categories – silver, china, glassware, collector books, and so forth. Then she had her three children draw straws to determine the selection from each category. The drawing rotated so that the one who drew the longest straw chooses first and went last for the following category. Others have created a point system so that each heir is allocated so many points and uses those points to bid on more valuable items or items that may be more valuable and important to them. Many of our clients use a lottery provision to direct the successor trustee in making these distributions.

We have clients who tag non-titled personal property items with recipients' names. We have clients who ask children to tag what they want. When more than one family member wants the same thing, they flip a coin until a recipient is determined. People get creative with this. They know their family. When a system or method of choosing is identified, it typically works well.

In creating a process, it is always good to remind heirs that if you have created a system that results in them receiving an item they did not necessarily want, they can always trade one or more of their items with someone else by mutual agreement.

We should also anticipate which items might be emotionally charged. Do not underestimate this. Acknowledging this reality allows you to address that issue in your plan. Ignoring this may create significant tension among your beneficiaries.

Do not ignore this issue. Bad behavior can ruin a good plan.

Do not forget family photos, movies, personal notes, and portraits. Most items can be digitized and widely distributed in today's digital world. However, someone will receive the original. We have witnessed severe family disagreements over who gets to retain the original photos. One family nearly disintegrated because of a dispute over who got to retain the original love letters their father sent their mother during wartime.

There are multiple considerations when considering the distribution of personal property. Everyone processes grief differently. That grief is not likely to emerge or become a point of discontent when a certificate of deposit is split into equal shares. There is clarity and little emotion to that distribution. This is frequently not the case when distributing items of personal property.

Your legal representative should be as transparent as possible and give beneficiaries an idea about the process of dividing and distributing personal items and how long it will take. Some beneficiaries want their spouses and children to be involved in the decision-making. That adds a level of complexity that may impede the process. I recommend only the heirs be present for any division process or in-person selections. Note: it seldom works out that way.

Distributing your personal property assets can be a quite-complex, emotionally-charged experience. We certainly did not cover all of them in this chapter. While there is no perfect solution, like all the other issues surrounding your estate plan, thoughtful consideration, anticipation, and declaring your intent during your lifetime will make the process easier for all parties.

Should You Consider
an Irrevocable Trust?

Earlier in the book, I said estate planning is all about asset protection. When I use the term "asset protection", I am speaking in a broader sense than asset protection as a strategy to mitigate creditor claims against your estate. The level of asset protection required, or desired, differs for each person. Some asset protection tools offer liability protection against creditor claims; others do not. For example, we now know that despite the many advantages of a revocable trust, it does not offer protection against the legitimate claims of creditors.

By contrast, an irrevocable trust offers asset protection opportunities not available in a revocable trust.

We know the revocable trust can be amended, modified, or changed at any time, right? So contrasted simply, the irrevocable trust technically means that you cannot change the terms of that document. You can continue to be the trustee of it. But you can't make changes to the document.

For example, you can't change the beneficiaries or who follows you as a trustee. At the surface level, that is the major difference between revocable and irrevocable.

Over time, strategies have been integrated into irrevocable trust planning, providing greater flexibility to modify an irrevocable trust. The use of a Trust Protector has long been established in international law. The Trust Protector is a person or party identified in the trust document who can make changes to an irrevocable trust on behalf of a trustor that the trustor cannot make themselves. Using of a Trust Protector has now made its way into planning in the United States.

We include Trust Protector language in all our trust agreements. In certain situations, the third-party Trust Protector can make changes the trustor cannot make themselves. This provides much more flexibility with an irrevocable trust than we had before.

In addition, some states have passed legislation allowing an irrevocable trust to be decanted or modified if certain conditions warrant a change to the terms of the trust. The trustee or Trust Protector is usually the party empowered to make these changes.

And then third, the parties can always go to court and ask for a judicial reformation of an irrevocable trust.

So, the irrevocable trust is not as harsh as it sounds in terms of it being locked into four square corners. With appropriate provisions, there is some flexibility to modify the terms of the irrevocable trust.

Recently, I was asked to make a guest appearance on a radio show. The host wanted me to discuss irrevocable trusts – what they are, how they are different from a revocable trust, and when their use would be appropriate in an estate plan. It occurred to me that the topic deserved a chapter in this book.

Terms that apply to the various types of irrevocable trusts are a sea of acronyms and labels. You will see acronyms such as ILIT, CRT, CLT, QPRT, SNT, MAPT, GRAT, Dynasty, and DAPT. All serve a purpose – to remove assets from your taxable estate for the benefit of another entity or other people.

> **When utilizing an irrevocable trust in your estate planning, you should seek very experienced and competent legal and tax counsel.**

All trusts – revocable or irrevocable - have the same three parties identified in the agreement. Trustors (grantor or settlor) are the parties who own the assets and create the trust. A trustee is named to manage the assets, and beneficiaries are designated to receive the benefits of the trust. In short, the money.

In a revocable trust, the trustor retains all incidents of ownership. Unless the trust indicates otherwise, the IRS treats the revocable agreement as a grantor trust. That means all assets continue to be attached to the trustor's Social Security Number and income from trust assets are reported on the trustor's personal 1040 tax return. For tax purposes, it's as if the revocable trust does not exist.

As previously discussed, a revocable trust can be amended, modified, or revoked in its entirety. All trust assets are included in the gross estate of the trustor for estate tax purposes, and the assets are available to the trustor's creditors. A revocable trust is not an asset protection strategy to escape liability from creditors. Other estate planning tools, such as an irrevocable trust, are available for that purpose.

How Does an Irrevocable Trust Work?

In contrast to a revocable trust, think of an irrevocable one as one that cannot be amended, modified, or revoked. As mentioned earlier, there are a few exceptions: if all beneficiaries agree; the trust is amended or decanted by the trustee or Trust Protector; or the trust is amended or decanted by judicial reformation.

From an income tax point of view, it gets a little tricky. As mentioned above, an irrevocable trust may be treated as a grantor trust with all income reported on the trustor's 1040 even though the trustor no longer owns the trust assets. Depending on the purpose of the irrevocable trust, it may be more tax-efficient to have the trust treated as a non-grantor trust.

In that case, income from trust assets is reported by the trust or distributed to beneficiaries who would then pay the tax. Most trustees will distribute income from the trust to beneficiaries because the tax rates of a trust kick in a much lower income level than individual tax rates. For example, in 2022, trust income is taxed at the highest tax rate when undistributed income reaches $13,450. Individuals are not taxed at the highest rate until their taxable income reaches $539,900 for a single filer and $647,850 for joint filers. In most cases, there is a significant tax incentive to distribute trust income to beneficiaries and let them pay the tax.

When a trustor transfers assets to an irrevocable trust they are removed from the trustor's estate for estate tax purposes. The transfer is considered a gift, one that requires filing a 709 Gift Tax return if the value of the transfer exceeds the current annual gift tax exclusion of $16,000.

When the trustor transfers assets into an irrevocable trust, they are relinquishing incidents of ownership. Because the trustor no longer owns the asset, it may eliminate exposing those assets to the claims of the trustor's creditors. There is always a discussion around whether transfers to an irrevocable trust offer protection from current and future creditors. That requires a more detailed analysis of state and federal law and the client's specific circumstances that extend beyond this book's scope. However, it is often a crucial matter for the client asking the question.

Now we know more about an irrevocable trust, what it is and how it works. When might someone want to utilize this type of trust as one of their estate planning options?

Clients utilize an irrevocable trust when they want to remove assets from their taxable estate to reduce or minimize estate taxes. The beneficiaries are typically their children and future generations or charities they support.

Suppose Stan and Betsy have accumulated assets with a net value exceeding their combined estate tax exclusions. They might want to remove those assets from their taxable estate so that the growth in the value of those assets escapes estate tax. They would create an irrevocable trust, have their assets appraised, transfer the property or asset to the irrevocable trust, and file a 709 Gift Tax return claiming the value of the asset against their lifetime gift and estate tax exclusion.

They might name their children and grandchildren as beneficiaries. They might designate a charity as the beneficiary. The asset and its future appreciation is no longer included in the taxable estate of either Stan or Betsy.

Irrevocable Trusts and Life Insurance

Another common use of an irrevocable trust is to shelter the death benefit of life insurance policies from estate taxation. Normally, the death benefit of life insurance is income tax-free. However, that death benefit is included in the policy owner's estate for estate tax purposes.

Assume a few years ago Stan purchased a $1 million insurance policy on his life. On the policy application, it would be a common practice to have Stan shown as the owner and insured. He would likely name Betsy as the beneficiary. As structured, Betsy's death benefit would not be subject to income tax. However, because Stan is the designated owner, the death benefit is included in his gross estate for estate tax purposes.

Suppose further that when creating their estate plan, we learn Stan and Betsy may be exposed to estate tax. We explore ways to remove the insurance policy death benefit from Stan's taxable estate. We recommend that Stan create an irrevocable trust (sometimes referred to as an "ILIT" for irrevocable life insurance trust) and transfer his life insurance policy ownership to the newly created ILIT. The ILIT will now be the owner and beneficiary of the policy. This can be done for an existing policy or a newly issued policy.

Care must be taken on the transfer of an existing policy because if the insured owner of the policy dies within three years, the value of the death benefit will be pulled back into their gross estate for estate tax purposes. Creating an ILIT to be the original owner and beneficiary of a newly issued policy will avoid the three-year inclusion issue.

Once the ILIT owns the insurance policy, the death benefit is removed from your taxable estate and is income-tax-free and estate tax-free.

Dynasty Trust Planning

I briefly mentioned this earlier but gave it no label. Another use of an irrevocable trust is to remove assets from your taxable estate and have the trust hold the assets for the benefit of children, grandchildren, and even more remote family beneficiaries. This kind of long-term irrevocable trust is often referred to as a Dynasty Trust because it was created to benefit future generations of your family, at least as far into the future as the law allows.

Again, assume Stan and Betsy want to remove assets from their estate to minimize future estate taxes. As discussed before, the same mechanics of creating the trust and filing the 709 Gift Tax return would apply. However, in this trust, Stan and Betsy want to have the trust assets benefit their children and future generations of their family. They structure the distributions so that an independent trustee has the discretion to distribute trust income and principal to beneficiaries of each generation for their health, education, maintenance, and support or what the IRS refers to as ascertainable standards. That restriction keeps trust assets from being included in the children's estates and the estates of future generations.

Stan and Betsy may also add additional conditions that must be satisfied before a beneficiary receives a distribution from the trust. An example would be passing a drug test or completing college. One of our clients stipulated that a beneficiary could not receive an annual distribution of trust income and principal above their adjusted gross income as reported on the beneficiary's previous year's 1040 income tax return.

An irrevocable Dynasty-type trust will remove assets from the gross estate of Stan and Betsy. Their heirs have the use and enjoyment of the assets during their lifetime, and the assets will not be subject to creditor claims.

If Stan and Betsy desire to benefit a charity, they might create an irrevocable charitable trust. A gift to an irrevocable Charitable Remainder Trust ("CRT") would remove the assets from their taxable estate and require filing a 709 Gift Tax return. The CRT can provide Stan and Betsy receive a stream of income from the CRT during their lifetime or for a term of years. Assets remaining in the CRT at their death are transferred to the charitable beneficiary designated in the trust. The gift of assets into the CRT will also create a charitable contribution deduction against their current income. Finally, when the CRT sells appreciated assets Stan and Betsy contributed, there are no capital gains taxes.

A Charitable Lead Trust ("CLT") works in reverse. With a CRT, the charity receives the balance of trust assets at the expiration of a term of years, or upon the trustor's death. In a CLT, the charity receives the immediate benefit of a revenue stream for a term of years or during the trustor's lifetime. Upon expiration of the term of years or the trustor's lifetime, the assets revert back to the trustor's family tax-free.

As with all irrevocable trust planning, the rules concerning how a CRT or CLT is structured, how income from the CRT or CLT is calculated, and what assets are appropriate for the trust to own require careful legal and tax planning. It can be complicated. You should always seek the advice of experienced legal and tax counsel.

Removing Your Personal Residence From Your Estate

Current law allows Stan and Betsy to transfer their personal residence to a Qualified Personal Residence Trust ("QPRT") to remove the value of their residence from their taxable estate. The QPRT is an excellent opportunity to utilize a portion of their lifetime estate tax exclusion painlessly and effectively. It is painless for Stan and Betsy because it does not involve using their cash or liquid assets and because the transfer of the home to the QPRT will have a minimal effect on them. They may continue to occupy the residence.

The requirements are the same as they are when creating an irrevocable trust. There is a valuation of the residence. A 709 Gift Tax return is filed. In the case of a QPRT, the return will reflect the use of your lifetime exclusion equal to the value of the residence, less the value of your lifetime right to occupy the home.

There is also a condition attached to the transfer of the home. The QPRT will contain a term of years that must be exceeded before the transfer of the home is considered complete. The asset will be completely removed from your estate and transferred to the beneficiaries only upon that meeting that condition. If the trustor dies before the term is reached, the homeownership is returned to the trustor.

The transaction is treated as if the transfer to the QRPT was never made for gift and estate tax purposes.

Say Stan and Betsy create a QPRT with a 10-year term. Only if they survive the term will the transfer of the homeownership be completed to beneficiaries.

Here is one caveat. Stan and Betsy's continued occupancy in the residence creates a split-interest gift. In other words, your occupancy's lifetime value reduces the residence's total value removed from the estate. IRS tables determine the lifetime value of your occupancy. Here is an example.

Assume Stan and Betsy are 60 years of age, the value of the residence is $500,000, and the term of years selected to complete the gift to children is ten years. For the transfer to be completed, Stan and Betsy must survive the 10-year term. However, the right to occupy the home during the 10-year term is treated as a retained interest and reduces the amount of the gift. Technically, the amount of the taxable gift reported on the 709 Gift Tax return is the total value of the property transferred less the actuarial value of the right to occupancy retained by the grantor.

According to IRS tables, based on our assumed value of Stan and Betsy's age of 60, a residence value of $500,000, and a 10-year term, the gift amount will be approximately $417,000. If the appreciation rate of the home is 4%, the value of the home when the term expires would be approximately $740,000. The transfer could mean a death tax savings of approximately $158,000. The transfer ends up being advantageous because the actuarial discounting based on the IRS tables will eventually transfer the home to children at a gift tax value of far less than the actual home value.

There are two other caveats to using a QPRT. First, during the term, the trustor is required to pay a fair market rent for their occupancy. Second, if the house passes to the children at the end of the QPRT term, their tax basis will be the same as the trustors. They will not receive a step-up in the tax basis of the residence at the death of Stan and Betsy.

When considering a QPRT, Stan and Betsy should consider their out-of-pocket costs and whether their potential estate tax savings outweigh the loss of a tax basis step-up for their children. In other words, will more estate taxes be paid if they retain the home in their estate, or will more taxes be paid by the children when they sell the house after their parents pass? And, future tax rates and the present value of those calculations must be considered.

The Grantor Retained Annuity Trust

If Stan and Betsy own assets they believe will experience a significant increase in value over a short number of years, Grantor Retained Annuity Trust ("GRAT") may be an attractive estate planning strategy. The GRAT is an advanced estate planning "freeze" strategy that allows appreciation in trust assets to be transferred to beneficiaries with little, if any, gift or estate tax consequences.

A GRAT is another form of an irrevocable trust used to make lifetime gifts of assets to beneficiaries while incurring little or no federal gift tax. A significant advantage of the GRAT over many other wealth transfer strategies is that a considerable body of regulations and favorable tax court rulings guide us on how to structure and operate a GRAT effectively.

Like the QRPT, the GRAT has a term of years. In the case of the GRAT, the term must be a minimum of two years. There is no limit on the maximum term.

If the trustor survives the GRAT term, the trust can pass the increase in value of trust assets to the children. The increase in value escapes inclusion in the grantor's estate. Like the QRPT, if the trustor dies before the trust terminates, the trust assets revert to the trustor's estate.

Like most trusts, the GRAT is structured as grantor trust meaning the trustor pays all of the tax on income earned by the Trust during the term. This trust is referred to as an "annuity" trust because following the transfer of assets to the trust, the trustor receives a set annuity payment from trust assets each year. An additional benefit of the GRAT is that the trustor does not pay tax on the annuity payments.

Annuity payments to the trustor may be made in cash or in-kind. If not enough cash is available when the annuity payment is due, the annuity payment can be made with stocks or bonds or any other assets held by the trust. In-kind payments may help avoid capital gains taxes that might be incurred if assets must be liquidated to make the annuity payment.

The key to the success of this strategy is to distribute the lowest possible annuity payments back to the trustor each year. The lower the required annuity payments to the trustor, the larger the value in the trust for the beneficiaries. The IRS Section 7520 interest rate determines the annuity payments. The amount of any gift tax that may be due is calculated by subtracting the present value of the trustor's retained interest from the value of the assets transferred to the trust. This estate "freeze" strategy works when the assets' growth during the Trust's term exceeds the Section 7520 rate. The excess amount can be distributed to the trust's beneficiaries, incurring little, if any, gift tax liability.

Planning For Children with Special Needs

Families who have children with special needs often create an irrevocable special needs trust ("SNT") for the benefit of that child to ensure there is no loss of government benefits the child may be receiving.

An SNT can be created as a first-party SNT or third-party SNT. It is important to determine which type of SNT you have or need. This depends upon whose property is funding the SNT. If the property funding the SNT originates with the SNT beneficiary, then it is a first-party SNT. However, if the property funding the SNT always belonged to someone other than the SNT beneficiary, then it must be drafted as a third-party SNT.

Like all irrevocable trusts, an SNT has specific rules that must be followed. Much depends on benefits the person is currently receiving. They may be receiving Medicaid, Supplemental Security Income ("SSI") benefits, or Social Security Disability Insurance ("SSDI") benefits. Many individuals are eligible for benefits under both programs at the same time. If a person receiving Medicaid benefits creates an SNT for their own benefit they will lose their Medicaid benefits.

The primary difference between the programs is that SSI determination is based on age/disability and limited income and resources. SSDI qualification is based on disability and work credits. In addition, in most states, an SSI recipient will automatically qualify for health care coverage through Medicaid.

Administering an SNT can be tricky. The trust is to provide *supplemental* needs only for the beneficiary, not money for essentials. This means the beneficiary with special needs cannot access the trust for health, support, or maintenance, nor can the trustee be obligated to provide for the beneficiary's health, support, or maintenance. This approach should prevent the special needs trust from being characterized as an available resource for the means-tested programs and should protect trust assets.

Perhaps the most important difference between third-party SNTs and first-party SNTs is what happens to SNT property when the beneficiary dies. Upon the beneficiary's death, the third-party SNT is not required to use the remaining assets to reimburse any state(s) for the Medicaid benefits received by the beneficiary during their lifetime. As a result, this type of SNT is a valuable planning tool for people who want to set aside property for a beneficiary with disabilities, preserve essential public benefits during that beneficiary's lifetime, and remain in complete control of where all of the remaining SNT assets will go upon the beneficiary's death.

What is a Domestic Asset Protection Trust?

Some states have created self-settled trusts called Domestic Asset Protection Trusts ("DAPT"). These irrevocable trusts are designed to protect your assets from the claims of future creditors. Notice, I said future creditors. They are not effective against existing claims. There may be challenges in protecting assets with a DAPT from existing creditors' claims.

The DAPT allows the trustor of the trust to retain access to some benefits of the trust while still protecting the assets from the creditor claims of the trustor. The requirements for a DAPT to be effective are precise. A few DAPTs have recently come under attack by courts. In one case, the court allowed a bankruptcy trustee to access trust assets because the assets were transferred to the trust less than ten years earlier.

The Medicaid Asset Protection Trust

This area of our practice is handled by our Elder Law Division and is quite complex. It deserves a book of its own. I cover the topic because people are concerned about the financial burden of long-term care in their declining years, whether that cost is incurred by entering a nursing home or from at-home care.

The average annual cost of a nursing home in the U.S. today exceeds $100,000. In our state, perhaps yours, the cost is somewhat less. In addition to the financial cost, the emotional cost can be devastating. Many people spend every last dollar they have, hoping to receive the best possible care in a nursing home.

If you enter a nursing home or need skilled care, there are only a few ways to pay for it. If you are a veteran, you may qualify for some assistance through the government's VA Aid and Attendance program. You may have purchased long-term health care insurance allowing you to lay off some, perhaps all, of your long-term care cost to an insurance company. Otherwise, you will pay for this cost out of pocket until death, or you recapacitate and return to your home. Here's what you should know.

Medicare will not pay for your nursing home care.

Qualifying for Medicaid benefits is either facilitated by pre-planning in advance of the need to enter a nursing home and satisfying the five-year look-back period, or crisis planning. This occurs when someone calls our office and tells us their father is entering a nursing home within the next few week or months. Then our focus is on minimizing the damage caused by spend down requirements before qualification occurs.

On the pre-planning side, one strategy, now being used more frequently, is creating an irrevocable trust to reposition assets in your estate so that you can qualify for Medicaid benefits more rapidly than you would if you held those assets in your own name or in the name of your revocable trust. We refer to these trusts as a Medicaid Asset Protection Trust ("MAPT").

Like other irrevocable trusts, the trustor transfers ownership of assets to the MAPT. The trustor is limited to what benefits they can receive from the trust during their lifetime, typically only the income generated by trust assets.

Medicaid rules were established by federal legislation. The federal law left it to the discretion of each state to implement and create its own rules about how to interpret the federal rules for purposes of qualifying for benefits. One sacrosanct federal rule is that applicants can only have $2,000 in assets in their name to qualify.

There is also a "look-back" period of five years. Medicaid will review any gifts or asset transfers you may have made during the past five years. If any, that will create a disqualification period expressed by the number of months you must pay for the nursing home with your own money before qualifying for Medicaid assistance.

Each state has "exempt" assets that a Medicaid applicant can retain without triggering a rejection of your application for benefits. Exemptions include personal belongings, household furnishings, an automobile, irrevocable burial trusts, and one's primary home. For home exemption, the Medicaid applicant must live in the home or have the intent to return to their home. In 2022, their home equity interest must be no more than $636,000. In addition to the asset tests, some states also have an income test and will reject an applicant if their income exceeds a specified amount each month, even if they meet the $2.000 asset test.

Creating a MAPT or repositioning assets to accelerate Medicaid qualification involves dealing with complex rules and legal strategies. If you are wondering how to prevent long-term health care costs from ravaging your assets, the assistance of an experienced elder law attorney is mandatory.

Tax Considerations and Estate Planning

There are always questions about how one's taxes might change and if there are any new requirements for reporting income taxes when creating an estate plan.

Income Taxes

There are no significant changes to your 1040 when creating your estate plan. If you choose a will as the foundation of your plan, it does not go into effect until your death. How you report your taxes and how your 1040 operates remains the same.

Likewise, if you choose a revocable trust as the foundation of your plan, there will be no changes in how you recognize and report income and expenses. The IRS says that a revocable trust is a grantor trust, and any income and deductible expenses are reported on your 1040 just as they were before creating the trust. You are still considered the owner of those assets for income tax purposes. There is no requirement to create a new Employer Identification Number ("EIN"). All assets will continue to utilize and be connected to your Social Security number.

With a revocable trust, gains and losses are subject to the same rules you are experiencing before creating a trust. The standard rules concerning the recognition of ordinary income or capital gains income from selling stock, investment property, mutual funds, or farmland remain the same. Losses incurred from the sale of those assets, depreciation expenses, and charitable contributions are reported in the same manner as you do before creating a trust, likewise, for your decision to itemize deductions or use the standard deduction.

In more complex transactions, the strategy might call for using a non-grantor trust. Now the rules and reporting have become more stringent. A non-grantor trust will be treated as a simple trust or a complex trust.

A simple trust is one where the income is distributed to beneficiaries each year. A complex trust is a trust that does not qualify as a simple trust. If categorized as a complex trust, certain requirements must be met. Each year the complex trust must either refrain from distributing all of its income to trust beneficiaries, distribute some or all of the principal assets in the trust to beneficiaries, or make distributions to charitable organizations.

Property Taxes

Each state has different laws about the impact of transferring ownership of your residence to your trust. Legal counsel should be able to guide you through those local rules. In addition to a deed and memorandum of trust, there are other forms to file in some states when transferring real estate to your trust. In most states, other than these unique form filing requirements, you should notice no change in your property taxes, at least no more or less than would have otherwise occurred.

Estate and Gift Taxes

In an earlier chapter, we discussed some of the rules concerning estate and gift taxes. Our coverage here reviews key points and helps reinforce the principles. When designing an estate plan, we always consider estate taxes, gift taxes, and generation-skipping taxes ("GST"). The estate and gift tax law is unified, meaning there is no distinction between what you gift to others during your lifetime and what you give them at the time of your death. Since 1976, both are all part of your taxable estate. What tax issues should be considered?

First is the estate and gift tax exclusion. The exclusion is defined as the amount of net asset value a person can give to any person without incurring estate tax liability. As of this writing (early 2022), the exclusion is $12.06 million per person. For a couple who has properly included appropriate tax planning into their estate plan, the available exclusions can be doubled to $24.12 million. This means you can pass more to your heirs today, without paying any federal gift or estate tax, than ever before in the past century. It also means most people do not have much current risk of incurring estate tax at death.

There is one caveat. The federal estate/gift exclusion for a married couple is available. It is not guaranteed. What does that mean? The exclusion is a use it or lose it proposition. A married couple must declare their use of both exclusions through proper estate tax planning. It does not happen by default. It does not automatically protect your opportunity to make tax-free estate transfers to your heirs. Losing the opportunity to utilize an estate tax exclusion means your family may be required to pay estate taxes they were not legally obligated to pay. All that is required to avoid this catastrophe is proper planning.

Here are a couple of quick examples. If you own the bulk of your assets as joint tenants with rights of survivorship when you die, your interest in those assets passes to the surviving joint tenant by operation of law. At that point, you have wasted your opportunity to declare to the IRS that you are utilizing all or part of your exclusion, so 50% of those assets would not be subject to estate tax.

Instead, the entire amount is included in the estate of the survivor, and the entire value is subject to estate tax at their death. If that amount exceeds the sole remaining exclusion, estate taxes are due. You lost an opportunity to shelter 50% of the value from estate tax and will now pay more than the law required.

The same would be true if your last will gives everything to your spouse at your demise and they fail to file a Form 706 Estate Tax return claiming the deceased spouse's exclusion through portability. Again, the risk is paying more in taxes than you are legally required to pay. Ouch!

What is the Annual Gift Tax Exclusion?

The second tax consideration is the annual gift exclusion. Today, the gift tax has a couple of clear rules. As of 2022, the annual gift exclusion is $16,000. You can make an annual tax-free gift up to that amount to anyone you choose and to as many people as you choose. The annual gift exclusion is adjusted for inflation each year. The exclusion is increased by $1,000 increments when the cumulative inflation adjustments call for the increase. If you make a gift over that amount, that gift would be subject to the gift tax and requires filing a Form 709 U.S Federal Gift Tax return.

If your gift exceeds the annual exclusion, and if you have a remaining balance on your lifetime estate and gift tax exclusion, the filing will not require an actual tax payment to the IRS. Instead, the 709 return triggers a reduction in your available lifetime exclusion.

Again, this rule follows a per donor-per-donee guideline. This means you can gift up to $16,000 to as many people as you wish during a calendar year. This rule offers significant planning opportunities in the right situation. Spouses can join in the gifting and double the annual exclusion up to $32,000 to as many donees as desired.

In addition, there are additional annual gift opportunities above the annual exclusion limits if the gift is made for education or medical purposes.

A simple example will illustrate how the annual gift exclusion works.

Assume Stan is a single person with two children. Further, assume a $1 million taxable estate we used earlier. Our friend Stan decides he wants to make a gift of $100,000 this year to each of his children. We know he can only make a tax-free gift of $16,000 to each child in any given year. Therefore $32,000 of the transfer will qualify for the annual gift exclusion. The remaining $168,000 would be subject to the gift tax.

We would file a U.S. Form 709 Gift Tax return, indicating Stan made a lifetime gift of $168,000 to his children. There would be no tax paid at the time of filing. Instead, the IRS would deduct $168,000 from his available lifetime exclusion.

The Generation-Skipping Transfer Tax ("GSTT")

Think of it this way. Currently, there are three potential taxes on a transfer of assets.

First, as we discussed, there is a gift tax on any transfer in excess of the annual gift exclusion.

Second, there is an estate tax on the excess amounts of your estate passed to heirs at your death that exceeds your remaining lifetime exclusion. Exceptions are transfers to spouses or charities.

Third, there is an additional flat GSTT on asset transfers to a person who falls into a skip generation.

At this point, the estate and gift tax laws are unified. That means that all gifts are treated the same over and above the annual gift exclusion, whether made during your lifetime or at your death. As I mentioned, any lifetime gift exceeding your annual exclusion is deducted from your available estate tax exclusion.

The GSTT is different. It is a separate add-on tax to estate tax and is triggered when a transfer of your assets is made to a skip generation. A skip generation would be your grandchild rather than your child. If you decide to leave assets to your children, your estate would be subject to estate tax on asset values in excess of the estate tax exclusion, and your children's estate would be subject to estate tax on asset values in excess of the estate tax exclusion at the time of their death.

If you leave assets to your grandchildren, your estate would be subject to estate tax if your assets exceed the exclusion amount, plus you would be subject to GSTT in addition to the estate tax.

There are additional rules about who is a skip person and what triggers the GSTT. These discussions must be held with an experienced estate planning attorney. The critical point is that there is a GSTT and it is a tax separate and apart from estate and gift tax.

This is an excellent example of why internet options and Legal Zoom are poor choices to help with our estate planning. No one is there to return your calls.

Discounting the Value of Your Estate

Follow me on this. The law says that assets you own are included in your estate for estate and gift tax purposes at their fair market value at the time of your death. A dollar bill is valued at $1. Gold is valued at its price per ounce. A stock is valued at the average between its high and low on the date of your death. A CD is valued at its face value. Farmland is valued at its appraised value. Same for all real estate. Tax authorities have formulas for valuing mineral interests. Privately owned businesses are valued by appraisal.

But what if your assets are transferred into a limited partnership ("LP") or limited liability company ("LLC") in exchange for you receiving an ownership interest in that entity? What do you now own at the time of your death? Correct, an interest in the LP or LLC. What if the operating agreement or partnership agreement imposes restrictions on your ability to sell your interest? Or limits your voting rights? Or restricts your rights to demand a return of your capital? What if you give away a portion of your ownership to your children so that you own less than 50% of the entity?

With those provisions in place, when you own less than 50% of the entity, you might be able to claim a minority discount in the value of your interest in the LLC or LP. In addition, due to the restrictions in the agreements, you might be able to deduct from that minority discount value an additional discount based on the lack of marketability of your interests. What buyer would want to purchase your 41% interest in an entity if they have little voting power, only have limited influence in the business and no control over the distribution of profits?

Discount planning transactions are very complex. They complicate your life because of the variety of entities created and the accounting that must be maintained. Independent appraisals of your LP or LLC establish the discounted value.

Estate tax returns that claim a discount in the value of the estate are often hotly contested by the IRS. They don't like the concept and have challenged several families in court who have attempted to reduce their estate tax liability through discount planning. There are winners and losers. Although the hurdles are high, the litigation has created a roadmap for correctly positioning a client's assets to garner this benefit. The taxpayer often loses because they did not operate the new entity as required. You cannot create a plan utilizing discounts, use it as your personal piggy bank, and expect to win the discount argument. It's not easy.

Look for the IRS to continue denying the benefits of discount planning. Some in Congress have suggested eliminating discount planning in recent tax proposals.

Other Tax Considerations

Another law stipulates that all assets you own at the time of your death are included in your taxable estate. Since your revocable trust is a grantor trust and since the IRS considers you the owner of those assets, all assets titled in the name of your revocable trust are likewise included in your taxable estate for estate tax purposes.

We also know you may transfer any amount to your spouse during your lifetime or at death without triggering a gift or estate tax liability. Of course, assets owned by your spouse at the time of their death will be subject to estate tax at their death.

Earlier, I discussed the concept of portability. A few years ago, the law expanded the use of our estate tax exclusion by allowing a spouse's unused estate tax exclusion to be ported or added to a surviving spouse's exclusion at the time of the survivor's death.

For purposes of making the calculations easier to understand, assume the exclusion is $12 million and that Stan dies first. Further, assume Stan's taxable estate was $8 million. Based on today's rules, we would file a 706 Federal Estate Tax return, claim usage of $8 million against his exclusion, and elect to "port" his unused $4 million to Betsy. If the exclusion remains the same at Betsy's death, she will have an available exclusion of $16 million to shelter her estate from tax liability.

What's So Important About 2026?

Because of today's high exclusion, most people don't have to worry about estate taxes. Be aware that current law stipulates that the exclusion sunsets on January 1, 2026, meaning the exclusion reverts to $5.49 million adjusted for inflation. The big takeaway is that the exclusion is coming down. More families will be exposed to sending 40% of their hard-earned money to Uncle Sam at the time of their death.

Today, people with a $10 to $12 million estate, for example, often believe they have no estate tax exposure with proper planning. Based on the current exclusion, they would be correct. After January 1, 2026, estate tax exposure may be in play again.

Another point of clarification. The estate tax is imposed on the net value of your estate after subtracting debt. Suppose the gross value of Stan's estate is $12 million and he has a $2 million mortgage against one of his real estate investments. The $2 million debt is subtracted from the gross value of the estate. Estate tax liability is based on the net fair market value of the estate.

When we use the term "gross value" of the estate, that is what is included in your estate for estate tax purposes. The "taxable estate" is the gross value of the assets less debt and other qualified deductions. The estate tax is calculated by applying the estate tax rate – currently 40% - to the taxable estate.

There are more tax considerations when planning an estate. This primer on the income, estate, gift, and GST basics will help you formulate a more detailed discussion with your estate planning attorney.

In a later chapter, there is more to say about proposed changes to our tax laws.

Now we will shift our conversation to estate planning for business owners.

Estate Planning for
The Business Owner

Estate planning becomes more complicated when a client owns a business, especially if some children are involved in the daily operations and others are not.

Let's create a scenario. In law school, we would call this a case study. Years ago, Stan acquired a few real estate investment properties. His banker mentioned a small manufacturing company for sale that was an excellent opportunity for someone. Stan went home, thought about it, and called his banker to see if he would work with him to acquire the company. The banker agreed to help secure financing through an SBA loan.

Stan acquires the company. As it often happens, acquiring the company was the easy part. Now Stan was personally obligated on a $3 million bank note. His real estate holdings were pledged as collateral. The monthly payments added to the intensity of his life. Thank goodness Betsy was on board with the decision. She was busy with her career pursuits. One involved another business that was proving highly successful. Both of them were responsible for raising their two wonderful teenage children.

If that was not enough, Stan now found himself immersed in the daily muck and mire of learning about manufacturing processes, internal operations, quality control, building a sales team, customer relationships, profit margin control, and growing the business. It was a load, and the first few years were touch and go. Yet, Stan focused and made it work. Profitability followed.

Stan's company operates in a relatively small industry space. Over the years, he acquired two of his competitors, both located in different states from the main operation. Economies of scale allowed the acquisitions to work out well.

After a few years, Stan needed help in one of the company divisions. Stan and Betsy's son, John, had carved out a nice career path in his own right. It happened to be in the area where Stan needed help. Eventually, John joins the company. Within a couple of years, John's capabilities and performance cause Stan to develop a high trust in him. Because of his ability, performance, and willingness, John assumes more responsibility in the company. A few years later, he became the Chief Operating Officer of Stan's company, responsible for the day-to-day operations. The company flourishes.

In another community, Stan and Betsy's daughter Susan was building a successful life of her own. Highly educated as a psychologist, Susan's career was on an upward trajectory. She met and married a terrific young man who recently left a large law firm to set up his practice. In time, they became parents of two incredible children.

As the company grew, Stan and Betsy approached me about their estate plan. As we discussed their questions, concerns, and goals, they made it clear that they wanted to be sure to distribute their estate to their children in equal shares, or at least as close to equal as possible.

This scenario occurs in many forms, in various business types, with multiple children, asset values, and other variables. It is not uncommon for the business to represent a significant percentage of a business owner's net worth. In many of these situations, one child may be working in the business; others are not. The child working in the business may play an essential role in helping grow the company's value. In many of these situations, the other children are in other professions, often in other cities.

Now the questions begin to emerge.

If you wish to distribute your estate to your children in equal shares, how do we accomplish that goal if your business represents a significant portion of your estate?

How do you value the business for the purpose of equalizing distributions to the children?

Depending on the value of the business, do we have estate tax issues to consider? If so, how will those taxes be paid? Is it possible the business or other assets will have to be sold to satisfy the estate tax liability? Do you force a sale of the business after your demise? What happens in Stan's case if John is committed to continuing to operate the business and does not want to sell?

What if John believes that because of his years of helping create value in the business, Stan and Betsy should leave 100% of the company to him?

What if John believes that because of his contribution to the company's value he should be "given" at least part of the business in addition to an equal distribution with his siblings?

Do you require that the children who are not involved in the business become part owners of the business with John? Is that what they want? Is that what John wants?

Do you require that the child in the business – John - buy out the interest of his siblings?

How will the buy-out be structured? And if so, does John have the cash or creditworthiness to buy out his siblings?

What if John cannot purchase the interest of his siblings? Would they agree to be John's banker and carry the purchase price in the form of a promissory note that pays them out over time? The siblings will surely want to retain their shares as collateral and secure his personal guarantee. They would probably want the personal guarantee of John's spouse.

Would the siblings prefer to be paid in cash? The answer is usually "Yes". Where would John get the cash? Would it be funded by an insurance policy on Stan's life, paid for by the company? At Stan's age, can the company afford the premium expense?

How does all of this relate to John's primary lender for his operating line of credit? The first thing to check is whether the bank has enough confidence in John to continue the operating line on the same terms and conditions afforded to Stan. Perhaps Stan has taken steps to ensure the bank's confidence in John's understanding of the business, his management skills, and financial acumen. Perhaps he has not. Even if the company's bank is confident about the transition of the business from Stan to John, they will evaluate the family's plan to ensure their collateral position is secure. They will likely require John's approval before moving forward.

We have to ask: does the child who's operating the business want a sibling as their banker? Does the sibling who is not involved in the business want to be their sibling's banker? Do they trust John to perform and pay them in full? As John's banker, what accountabilities will the siblings require?

These questions, and others, arise when creating an estate and succession plan for a business owner. It is a near certainty that the child involved in the business will develop strong opinions about what they should receive, when they should receive it, and how they should receive it.

They may believe that because they have been there and helped add value to the business, they should be given 100% of the business, and their siblings can take whatever remains in the estate.

That may not sit well with siblings who are not involved in the business. And, it will likely not square with Stan and Betsy's desire to share their estate equally with both children.

There are instances where the child involved in the business – John, for example – develops an entitlement mentality about ownership of the business. They might say, "I've worked for less money than I could have made on the outside. I could have taken a job with someone else and made more money. I deserve the business."

The non-involved siblings might respond by saying, "Why didn't you take that other job? If that opportunity was out there, then why didn't you take it?"

Can you hear the thoughts? "I've worked here for 20 years, sacrificed, helped build this company, and could have made more working for someone else than I made working in this company. I deserve to have this company."

Can you hear it?

If John has that mindset, it can make the estate and business succession more challenging. Everyone must understand that when a child is involved in the family business, there is a distinction between the child's employee/executive role and what they may receive as a beneficiary of the estate.

> **There is a distinction between working as a compensated employee in a family business and being a beneficiary of an estate that owns the company.**

As an employee – whether in the role of a janitor or Chief Operating Officer - John is providing a service to the company. He receives compensation for that service. Whether that compensation is fair, reasonable, or sufficient can be discussed. In his mind, John believes he is underpaid. His siblings are sure he is overpaid. That said, Stan offered John an opportunity and John voluntarily accepted it. And he chose to continue working in the business.

Those issues complicate succession and estate planning for a business owner. The transfer of ownership of a closely held business, whether to a family member, the management team, or a third party, is complex. The process requires an extensive investment of time, attention, and consideration of the family's goals, while the client is living and after they have passed away.

Here is one final point. I have already covered this, yet it bears repeating.

It is quite common for a company to have an operating line of credit to handle temporary short-term cash flow issues. The operating line of credit is typically secured by some combination of the company's accounts receivable, inventory and other assets. When Stan and Betsy are out of the picture, if the company has debt, the banker likely had a longstanding relationship with Stan and Betsy. They may not feel the same about loaning money to John, even though he has been working in the business for some time and has assumed many management responsibilities.

How would these issues impact the estate plan?

It will likely lead to a re-negotiation of the terms and conditions of the operating loan. Prudence requires Stan and Betsy to prepare for these contingencies carefully. The strategic plan for their business would include helping John develop a trusting and confident relationship with the banker. Doing this while living, documenting these steps in their estate plan, and establishing good governance policies within their company, enhances the odds of a successful – and profitable - transition of ownership of their business.

Let's discuss some of the strategies that can be utilized in planning for a business owner that helps solve many of these issues.

The Buy-Sell Agreement

Buy/sell agreements certainly have a seat at the table. These agreements are utilized when there is more than one business owner. Buy/sell agreements can be implemented for any business type, whether for shareholders of a regular corporation, members of a limited liability company, or partners in a partnership.

Buy/sell agreements are effective in any of those entities and can also be helpful when the parties have been together for an extended period or an older owner wants to bring in a younger successor and formalize how the transfer of ownership will occur.

Here is a basic overview of the mechanics.

Assume Stan and Rich are partners in their business. Stan owns a slim majority of the company. They organized the business in a traditional corporation and filed taxes as a C-corporation. For years, they have each operated within clear boundaries of responsibility. They agreed to reach a consensus on major decisions. It has worked well, and the business has prospered.

In this case, Rich is not a family member. The principles surrounding the buy/sell agreement are essentially the same if the co-owner is a family member. The fundamental question is, what happens if a co-owner becomes incapacitated or dies?

The share of the business owned by the disabled or deceased co-owner certainly has some value. His family certainly believes it does. Now the questions shift.

With no written agreement, what obligation does the remaining shareholder have to purchase the interest of the deceased shareholder? If the deceased owner's trust or will bequeathed his interest in the business to his spouse, will the remaining owner want the spouse as a new partner? What contribution will the surviving spouse make to the business? Now that the surviving spouse is an owner, will they sign a personal guaranty agreement with vendors or bankers on operating lines of credit? Or real estate loans? Probably not. You can see how these issues would lead to an impasse and perhaps a deterioration in the relationship.

A buy/sell agreement provides a roadmap for the purchase of the deceased shareholder's interest in the company. The agreement stipulates what events trigger the buyout. Triggers include death, disability (mental and physical), and even disappearance. Other terms address what occurs if a shareholder working in the business is terminated.

The agreement addresses the terms and conditions of the buy-out, including how the buy-out will be valued and funded.

Sometimes the parties decide to have the value determined by a third-party appraiser. In other instances, valuation is determined by a formula. For example, appraisers often set a value based on a multiple of earnings adjusted for taxes, depreciation expense, and amortization of loans. This is sometimes referred to as EBITDA. In other businesses, the values may rest more on multiples of gross revenue. Other factors may be included in determining valuation, such as adding a premium to the price due to a shareholder owning majority control or discounting the value for a minority position.

Once the valuation issue is resolved, the question then is, how will the purchase be funded? In other words, how will the family of the deceased or disabled shareholder be paid?

Rarely does the company have idle cash laying around to write the family a check for the full price. Using the company's liquid assets for the purpose might violate specific covenants the owners have with their lenders. The bank may advance additional monies to fund the purchase depending on the company's financial strength and cash flow.

That leaves two prevalent methods of funding the purchase. The first is through a promissory note by the remaining owner payable to the family. The second is using life insurance to provide the liquid funds to immediately complete the buyout. In some transactions, it is a combination of both. There are advantages and disadvantages to each method.

If a promissory note is used, the remaining shareholder promises to pay the family a certain amount each year, plus interest, until the obligation is satisfied. In effect, the family of the deceased is serving as the remaining shareholder's banker. The shares are worth a certain amount, the agreement stipulates the remaining shareholder will pay it, and the buy/sell stipulated the payout would occur over a certain period of time. If and how the loan will be collateralized is always a point of discussion. Will the remaining shareholder be obligated to personally guarantee the payment, or is this a company-only obligation? You are probably starting to see many twists and turns in this arrangement.

When using life insurance to fund the purchase, the death benefit amount is often linked to an agreed-upon valuation method. Too many attorneys overlook the use of life insurance in estate planning, especially in the context of succession planning for a business owner. The challenge is that the life insurance discussion often occurs too late when the age of the business owner or partners makes insurance too expensive.

> **Life insurance can provide liquidity for the purchase of the business, estate taxes, equalizing distributions to siblings, or debt reduction.**

When using life insurance, the purchase can be structured as a cross-purchase arrangement, an entity purchase agreement, or a hybrid of the two. Regardless of the method, the family receives a lump sum from a death benefit on the deceased's shareholder's life.

In the cross-purchase structure, the shareholders purchase insurance on one another's lives. Stan buys life insurance on Rich's life, and Rich buys insurance on Stan's life. The amounts will vary based on ownership. When a death occurs, the remaining shareholder is the beneficiary of the death benefit. The remaining shareholder then uses the proceeds they receive to pay the family in exchange for the family transferring the deceased's shares to the remaining shareholder.

With the entity purchase, the company buys the policies on Stan and Rich. The company is the owner and beneficiary of the policies. Were Rich to die, the company would receive the death benefit and uses the proceeds to purchase the shares from Rich's estate. Rich's shares are redeemed and retired.

When deciding which insurance structure to use, there are numerous variables and considerations, including the age of the owners, how the company is taxed, and how to protect the insurance proceeds from being included in one of the owner's taxable estate. Again, this is where Legal Zoom and other online options fail, and using the expertise of estate and tax attorneys pays big dividends.

Equalizing Estate Distributions to Children

Most – not all, but most – of our clients tell us they want to distribute their estate to the children in equal shares, or at least as close to equal as possible. It is also common for a business owner client that the value of their business represents more than 50% of their estate. If not all of the children are involved in the business, how do we solve this Rubik's cube of a challenge and split the estate into equal shares?

Again, assume the business comprises more than 50% of Stan and Betsy's net worth. If their estate plan calls for the children to receive everything in equal shares, that means Susan will own at least part of the company, even if John receives the company as his entire 50% share and Susan receives the house and all other assets.

Susan could decide to be a minority co-owner with her brother. If she is not working in the business, the only consistent benefit she might receive would be dividends, but only if and when John decides to declare them. Family advisors often overlook how this arrangement might impact the relationship between John and Susan. If they have a great relationship, might this create tensions not experienced before? What are the chances of this arrangement exacerbating an already tenuous relationship if they are not close? What about the attitude of

John and Susan's spouses? They have a role in how the workability of these arrangements.

Susan likely wants John to buy her shares. How would he arrange that? He received the company stock as his 50% share. Where would John get the cash? If he has limited access to funding, and if the bank will not loan him the money to purchase Susan's shares, perhaps she will agree to have him sign a promissory note and pay her over time. As we saw before, even that can get awkward.

As an alternative, insurance can play a role in this situation. Stan purchases a policy on his life and names a trust as the beneficiary. Upon his death, the trust uses the proceeds to help equalize the estate distribution to the children. There are nuances to how this might be structured. Family relationships, affordability, income tax issues, and estate tax consequences must be considered. Yet, the concept shows how clean and straightforward this insurance strategy might be in this situation.

This chapter fails to do service to the topic. There are so many issues and topics remaining that we did not have the chance to cover in the limited space of this chapter. Transitioning ownership of a business is jam-packed with challenges. If Stan and Betsy fail to consider these issues, problems may impact the business, its team members, and family relationships forever. A revocable trust alone will not solve these challenges. As I said before, anytime a family business is involved in estate planning, it is always a more complicated and complex journey. There are many moving parts. Planning for a business owner requires experienced estate and tax counsel.

So does planning for farm and ranch clients. Let's take a look.

Farm and Ranch Planning

M any of the issues arising with farm and ranch families are similar to those experienced by owners of family businesses.

Again, assume Stan and Betsy own a farm and ranch operation consisting of 750 acres of tillable land for corn and soybeans and 500 acres of grassland for a cow-calf operation. If they lived in a wheat-producing state, they might own 1,000 – 2,000 acres, even more, of wheat land and a few hundred acres for their cow-calf operation. They own the typical farm portfolio of tools, machinery, equipment, vehicles, and feed. They own the minerals on some, but not all, portions of their land. Assume Betsy inherited some minerals from her parents.

Stan and Betsy have two children – John and Susan. John is married with two children. He has been working side by side with Stan on the farm for years. Stan and Betsy surveyed and carved out a two-acre piece of the land and deeded it to John so he could build his family home close to them. In addition, John has acquired land of his own and has a substantial operation in his own right. Susan is a teacher, wife, and mother in the nearest large city. She has no interest in the farming operation.

The love relationship between and among Stan, Betsy, John, and Susan is strong. Everyone gets along for now.

In terms of the day-to-day operations, things get a little hazy from time to time. John often fills up his pickup and tractors with gas from the tank at Stan's place. Stan uses John's equipment from time to time. When they purchase feed, salt, fencing material, or fertilizer, it often ends up homogenized and shared in some form or fashion between John's operation and Stan's. When extra labor is needed, sometimes Stan pays for it. Other times it falls on John's account. The accounting is not extremely clean.

They say, "…it all works out in the end." Imagine sorting all this out each year for tax purposes.

A variation of this fact pattern might be that neither of Stan and Betsy's children is involved in their farming operation. One might be interested in keeping ownership of the farm in the family name. The other could care less.

Like planning for the owner of a closely-held business, the farm and ranch estate planning process becomes more complicated when you have two or more children, one involved in the operation and the other not. As with planning for owners of family businesses, questions begin to emerge. We continue to hear from Stan and Betsy that they want to split the estate as equally as possible.

What if Stan and Betsy think they want to give each child specific tracts of land rather than give each child an equal fifty percent (50%) interest in the entire farm as tenants in common?

What if the tracts one child receives have underlying minerals, and the land the other child receives owns no mineral interests?

If they split everything equally, what in the world will Susan do with a plow and old combine in the city? Or, with 50 momma cows who will calve during February?

If there is a 50-50 tenant in common ownership split, will Susan lease her interest back to John for him to operate in exchange for an annual cash rent arrangement? Or will they create a "sharing" arrangement where Susan contributes her portion of the land, John contributes equipment and labor, and they split seed, fertilizer, and other expenses in some fashion? John has never been required to pay rent for the privilege of farming this tract of land before.

How does John feel about having to lease Susan's interest in the farm? What if he refuses?

Even if John agrees to cash rent lease the land, can he afford to pay Susan the fair market rental rate on the lease?

What happens if they cannot agree on a fair price?

What if Susan wants to be bought out? Assuming they agree on the price, can John arrange financing to complete the purchase?

If he cannot, will Susan agree to be John's banker by selling her one-half interest to him for a small down payment and the balance evidenced by a promissory note paid out over a period of years and secured by a mortgage on the land?

Does Susan trust John to meet these obligations?

What about the mineral interests and revenue that might come from producing oil or gas wells? How do they get divided? Equally, or do the minerals follow the surface and benefit only the child who receives land with minerals attached?

Grab the Rubik's cube again. How do we resolve these issues? What is reasonable? In whose opinion? What is acceptable to both parties? I hesitate to use the term "fair" because that word carries a significant amount of emotional baggage, and misapplied can be disruptive.

What's fair to one person may not be fair to another. To me, the better term is workable. The better question is, what is required to make this plan workable going forward?

Farm and ranch operators commonly have bank loans or loans through some other ag lender. They may have an entity such as a limited liability company ("LLC") that owns the land and buys equipment, seed, cattle, or equipment. Sometimes the land is in a separate LLC.

The goal of virtually every farm and ranch client we have is to pay off the land to own the land free and clear as soon as possible. Many make years-long sacrifices to ensure that outcome.

That is why farm and ranch operators often say they are cash poor and land-rich. They have worked an entire lifetime and delayed spending gratification to pay off the debt on the land.

It is not uncommon, though, for them to still have a cattle loan, or they may have an equipment loan, or they may have a bill at the feed store or with the fertilizer company at the time of their death.

As in a family-owned business, the question emerges again when settling the estate, particularly concerning John taking over the operation. Will the vendors, the bankers, the feed companies, and the grain elevators be willing to extend the amount of credit to John that they extended to Stan and Betsy? Effective estate planning requires the answer to be yes. That happens only if Stan and Betsy think forward to ensure these business relationships seamlessly transfer to John.

There must be a plan. Effective estate planning must always work toward reaching the family goals. One of those often-overlooked goals is preserving the integrity of the family unit and doing everything possible to ensure relationships flourish.

Most of the time, there is little, if any, thought given to these issues. Or, if there is a thought about it, the process seems overwhelming. Nothing gets done. The result is considerable stress within the family unit. If John is not as well thought of in the community or has a weak relationship with bankers or other vendors, we often help families navigate those matters.

It should be clear that when planning for farm and ranch families, the emotional leg of the estate planning stool is as important as the legal, tax, and financial legs.

When planning for our farm and ranch clients, we must consider estate tax issues. Farm and ranch families – yes, you know who you are – are notorious for claiming "we don't have much" or thinking the value of their operation is what they paid for it, often decades earlier. We often have to tune them into the estate tax reality show.

In our state, we also have farm and ranch owners who have producing oil and gas interests on their land. There are a few cases where lease bonus payments to the landowners exceeded the value of the land! Then, if the drilling is successful, the revenue stream from oil and gas production must be valued and added to the owner's gross estate for estate tax purposes.

Overall, the same principles apply here that we discussed in the chapter on planning for business owners.

Any business owner, or a farm and ranch owner, should work with an experienced estate planning attorney who has years of experience helping families navigate these murky waters. There are far to many variables for them to leave to chance or try to handle themselves.

What About My Retirement Accounts?

Planning for retirement accounts deserves this separate chapter. When making decisions about retirement accounts, there are income tax, estate planning, and financial planning implications. This is one area where income tax planning, retirement planning, and estate planning intersect. The rules governing retirement accounts are complicated, complex and difficult to sort through, even with a slide rule or calculator. You need an Artificial Intelligence machine. Yet, understanding a few basics will help you make informed decisions and avoid costly mistakes.

Background

At the risk of sounding somewhat technical, Section 401(a)(9) of the IRC contains an income tax rule that governs minimum required distributions from qualified profit sharing, 401(k), pension, stock bonus plans, and section 403 annuity contracts. IRC Regulations also make this section applicable to IRAs, 403(b) tax shelter annuities, and section 457 deferred compensation plans of government and tax-exempt organizations.

If you have multiple accounts, plans, and IRAs, the minimum required distribution rules apply separately to each plan or IRA you maintain.

One benefit of these accounts is that if they are structured to receive pre-tax contributions, the assets accumulate value on a tax-deferred basis. Using pre-tax contributions means you can reduce your current taxable income by the contribution amount. The tax deferral is offset by the fact that 100% of all future distributions from the retirement account are taxed as ordinary income when received.

What is a Roth Retirement Account?

In contrast to the traditional pre-tax retirement account I just described, you may contribute after-tax money to a retirement account. With the passage of the Employee Retirement Income Security Act ("ERISA") in 1974, taxpayers were allowed to create what we know today as traditional, pre-tax IRAs. In 1997, Congress passed the Taxpayer Relief Act ("TRA"). I know, it is difficult to believe Congress would pass legislation offering taxpayers "relief."

The TRA created Roth retirement accounts, named after the U.S. Senator, William V. Roth, who sponsored the legislation. The distribution and tax rules are considerably different. This new type of retirement account allows taxpayers to invest already-taxed income into a retirement account that they or their heirs could withdraw tax-free.

Roth IRAs follow all the same rules that apply to traditional IRAs except for these notable distinctions:

- There are income limits that if exceeded, limit the ability to create a Roth. These limits apply to the type and amount of income received.
- Roth IRA contributions are not allowable tax deductions.
- If you have earned income, there is no age restriction on how long you may contribute to a Roth IRA
- Roth IRA accounts do not carry a requirement for mandatory withdrawals. Account owners can leave the funds in their account for their heirs.
- Whereas traditional IRA distributions are taxable when received, if you have held your Roth IRA for at least five years and you're older than age 59 1/2, Roth earnings during the holding period and distributions are tax-free to the account owner and their heirs.

It should be noted that the balance of your Roth account is still included in your taxable estate for estate tax purposes.

Distribution Rules

There are rules governing withdrawals that must be taken from your retirement accounts. With a few exceptions, the distributions are tied to your age. Once you reach a specific age, there is a minimum distribution requirement. We know those rules as the Required Minimum Distribution ("RMD") rules.

From an estate planning perspective, retirement assets are included in your taxable estate for purposes of determining your estate tax liability. These accounts are transferred to a designated beneficiary upon the account owner's death. Even though these accounts remain titled in your individual name, the contractual transfer to your beneficiary will not trigger probate of that asset.

If you are using a revocable trust as the foundation of your estate plan, you do not transfer ownership of retirement assets into the name of your trust like other titled assets. Title to retirement assets remain in your individual name. One very important variable is how you designate beneficiaries for retirement accounts. Mistakes can occur. Here is a closer look.

Over time, Congress created several rules regarding how retirement accounts operate. First, they are set up so they self-liquidate over your life expectancy. Second, there are penalties for the early withdrawal of money from these accounts. If you take distributions before age 59 1/2 there is a 10% penalty tax on the withdrawal. You pay tax on the withdrawal at your ordinary income tax rate plus a 10% penalty.

Before 2019 you were required to start taking RMDs no later than the year following the year in which you reached age 70 1/2. Once distributions commence, you are required to take a minimum distribution based on the principal amount of your IRA balance the previous December 31 and your remaining life expectancy according to IRS tables.

You are always able to withdraw more than your RMD.

In 2019 Congress made significant changes to some of the rules concerning the distributions from IRAs and retirement accounts.

The SECURE Act

The SECURE Act was passed and signed into law in December, 2019. The Act made several changes. Because there are numerous details and vital financial, tax, and estate considerations in the planning and management of retirement accounts, I encourage you to seek professional advice to ensure you are maximizing the benefits and avoiding costly mistakes. Here are a few of the basic rules.

For account owners, RMDs now begin the year the owner reaches age 72. The RMD must generally be withdrawn by December 31 of the RMD year. An exception applies to a first year RMD, which can be taken by the required beginning date ("RBD"). The amount you must withdraw depends on the balance in your account and your life expectancy as defined by the IRS tables.

> **It is the responsibility of the IRA owner to ensure RMD distributions are taken as required by law.**

Extending the RMD to age 72 means account owners will not have to take out a distribution as early as they did before the SECURE Act. Now your money to sit in the IRA account a little longer so the interest and earnings can continue to compound. This change was good news.

If Stan as the IRA account owner fails to take his RMD amount by the deadline, a penalty of 50% of the shortfall is owed to the IRS (excess accumulation penalty). This penalty also applies to beneficiaries with inherited accounts

If an employer-sponsored retirement plan allows it, the RMD can be deferred past age 72 until retirement unless you own more than five percent of the company's stock.

When does your RMD go into effect? April 1 of the year that follows the year the account owner reaches age 72 (age 70 ½ for those who reached age 70 ½ before 2020). For example, Stan reached age 72 in 2021. His RBD is April 1, 2022. Stan must take his first RMD for 2021 as late as April 1, 2022. For employer-sponsored retirement plans, the RBD would be April 1 of the year that follows the year of retirement, if the plan allows deferral of RMDs past age 72.

We are often asked, when is the best time to take the first RMD? Remember, only the first year's RMD can be deferred to the next year. Again, assume Stan reached age 72 in 2021. He can defer his first RMD until the RBD in April of 2022. It might be wise for him to consider the tax impact of electing (or not electing) such a deferral option. If Stan defers the RMD to 2022, it will mean he has to include two RMDs in his income for 2022. Everyone should consult with a tax professional to determine whether it makes good tax sense to defer the RMD amount or withdraw the amount in the year it is due.

Under the new SECURE Act if you have earned income, there's no age cap for contributing to a traditional IRA. Previously you had to stop the year you turned age 70½. This was good news.

The rules remained consistent on other points. For example, if you have more than one IRA, you can take a distribution from each account, or you can calculate the RMD for each account and take the entire distribution from one or more of the accounts.

Early Withdrawal Exceptions

There are some exceptions to the rules, meaning various situations may qualify you for an exception to the higher penalty tax on early withdrawals.

Exceptions to the early withdrawal penalty occurs if:

- An early withdrawal is used to pay for medical expenses if those expenses exceed 7.5% of your adjusted gross income;
- You are unemployed and use the withdrawn money to pay your medical insurance premiums;
- You are disabled;
- You withdraw funds from an inherited IRA received from a non-spouse;
- The funds are used to pay for qualified higher education expenses for yourself, your spouse, or the children or grandchildren of you or your spouse;
- You use up to $10,000 of the withdrawn money to buy, build, or rebuild a first home for yourself, a parent, grandparent, spouse, or for a child or grandchild of you or your spouse, or;
- You are a qualified reservist called into active duty.

Section 72(t) Withdrawals

There is also an exception to the early withdrawal penalty if the withdrawals qualify for an Internal Revenue Code Section 72 (t) Substantially Equal Periodic Payment ("SEPP"). If you elect to receive a SEPP payment from your IRA, you must withdraw the money according to a *specific schedule*. The IRS gives you three different methods to calculate your specific withdrawal schedule.

When you elect the Section 72(t) option and begin taking SEPP payments, you must continue with that specific payment schedule for five years or until you reach age 59 1/2, whichever comes later (unless you are disabled or die). For example, if you begin using the SEPP method at age 52 1/2 (seven years before you turn age 59 1/2), you must continue using the payment plan you established until you reach age 59 1/2. If you begin using the SEPP method at age 57 (2.5 years before you turn 59 1/2), you must follow that payment plan for five years or until you reach age 62.

If you deviate from your schedule before the appropriate amount of time has passed, the IRS will impose a penalty tax on *all* amounts you have withdrawn up to that point.

If you meet the 72(t) requirements, there will be no penalty imposed on the distributions. Another option allows you to withdraw a set amount of a 72 (t) payment each year based on your life expectancy. There are other rules to follow concerning these distributions. Consult your legal or financial advisor to help you navigate these rules and the available withdrawal options.

We have covered some basic rules regarding distributions from retirement accounts during your lifetime. Now we turn to a discussion about what happens in the event of your death.

The Importance of the Beneficiary Designation

This section examines options if a spouse is named as the primary beneficiary. The next section will explore the implications of naming a non-spouse as the primary beneficiary.

When setting up a retirement account, you are presented a beneficiary designation form, typically from your financial advisor. It is almost always completed with little, if any, consideration for your estate plan. On occasion, the form is completed for you. In other instances, the advisor will send you the form to complete.

It is important to remember that these change of beneficiary forms offer you the opportunity to designate a primary beneficiary and a contingent or secondary beneficiary. Both options should be completed.

> **When setting up your retirement account, remember to select both a primary and contingent beneficiary.**

One important point. Your spouse may not be entitled to receive your IRA simply by virtue of your marriage. The IRA will go to the person(s) contractually named as the primary beneficiary on the account. This outcome has some limitations, for example, in community property states. All assets acquired during marriage are considered to be owned equally in those states. Therefore, all contributions to an IRA are considered community property, and the surviving spouse would be entitled to one-half of the account, regardless of how the beneficiary designation is set up.

What happens if a surviving spouse is not satisfied with what they inherit? In virtually all states, they can go to court and claim their statutory elective share. That amount varies by state. Most courts will consider IRA funds when determining how much the survivor can claim. Let's return to the importance of the beneficiary designation.

If you have a spouse or partner, they will seem the obvious choice to be named the primary beneficiary. If your spouse is named as the primary beneficiary and you predecease him or her, they have options regarding how your IRA will be handled. How do the rules apply to our married couple, Stan and Betsy? Assume Stan is 74 and Betsy is 68. Betsy is designated as the primary beneficiary on Stan's IRA.

First, Betsy can elect to cash in the account balance and pay the federal and state taxes. The distribution will be taxed at ordinary income tax rates with the IRS and at the state level. Although this is an option, the distribution might elevate Betsy into a higher tax bracket. Depending on the tax rates in the state where Stan and Betsy reside, taxes might take up to 40% of the distribution. The good news is that there are no penalties against Betsy if she elects this option, regardless of her age.

Second, Betsy may elect to keep Stan's IRA in place and simply treat herself as the beneficiary. This option requires some analysis. Stan's age will determine Betsy's RMDs at the time of his death. At that point, we must consider whether Stan had reached age 72 and whether he was taking RMDs.

Since Stan was 74 at the time of his death, he was taking RMDs. With this option, Betsy's distributions will be based on Stan's life expectancy based on the RMD that was in place for him at the time of his passing or the single life expectancy of Betsy as the surviving spouse.

If Stan had died before reaching age 72 and he was not taking his RMDs, then Betsy can defer distributions until the date Stan would have been required to take RMDs. At that point, Betsy can take the remaining distributions over her single life expectancy.

This option appears to be best suited for a surviving spouse under 59 ½ or older than the deceased spouse.

The third option is for the surviving spouse to implement what is referred to as a spousal rollover. Only a surviving spouse can elect this option. The surviving spouse may either name themselves the owner of the IRA account or roll it into their own IRA account. Be sure the IRA custodian or trustee knows where to transfer the money. If they send you a check and you deposit it into your own IRA account, you may receive a serious frown from the IRS.

Let's apply the rollover strategy to Stan and Betsy. With this option, Betsy is now the IRA account owner after electing the rollover option. Betsy's RMDs will be based on her age beginning with the year in which she became the account owner, not the age of Stan, the deceased spouse. In our example, Stan started taking his RMDs when he reached 72. Betsy is 68. With the rollover option, there is a reset of the RMD clock, and Betsy can defer RMDs from the IRA until she reaches 72.

The advantage of this option is the continued deferral of income tax. If the surviving spouse has reached age 59½, they may take distributions without penalty. If they take distributions before reaching age 59½, they will be subject to the 10% penalty tax on the withdrawal amount.

The rollover option is best suited for a surviving spouse who is under 59½ years of age, or the deceased spouse was the older of the two.

Why is the contingent beneficiary important? Occasionally, we see people fail to designate a contingent or secondary beneficiary when establishing their retirement accounts. If your primary beneficiary predeceases you, and you have failed to name a contingent beneficiary, the default beneficiary becomes your "estate".

Whether by design or oversight, when your estate is the beneficiary, the probate-free contractual transfer of the IRA is lost. The IRA is subject to probate. You always want to name a contingent or secondary beneficiary on any retirement account. In fact, the principle applies to annuities and life insurance as well.
Those assets also transfer by the contractual provisions in the policy.

What are the rules when a non-spouse is named as the beneficiary of an IRA?

What is an Inherited IRA and How Does It Work?

Technically, all IRAs are "inherited" IRAs. The only exception is the spousal rollover option we discussed earlier. The most significant change under the SECURE Act is that a beneficiary of an inherited IRA can no longer "stretch" distributions over their life expectancy.

Under the previous rules, when someone inherited an IRA, say a child or grandchild, they could utilize the IRS tables and "stretch" the distributions over their remaining life expectancy. That is no longer possible. Under the SECURE Act, the beneficiary must take distributions out within ten years from the account owner's death date. No specific annual distributions are required; however, the entire balance must be taken by the end of the ten-year term.

In other words, you could leave the entire balance in the account for ten years to maximize tax-deferred account growth. If you choose that strategy, you will pay income tax at ordinary tax rates on the whole distribution. As I mentioned at the beginning of this chapter, planning for retirement accounts must consider retirement planning, income tax planning, and estate tax planning.

It was a significant advantage when non-spousal beneficiaries could take distributions from an inherited IRA out over their lifetime. It provided a lifetime revenue stream for a person who inherited the IRA. It also allowed more money to sit in that account, compound, and grow on a tax-deferred basis. If the IRA account grew 8% each year and the effective withdrawal rate was 4%, you can see that this arbitrage would add more money to the account over time.

The SECURE Act represents a significant change when considering intergenerational tax planning and saving taxes for multiple generations.

The SECURE Act of 2019 further modified the planning and distribution options for inherited IRAs. Now beneficiaries are either Designated Beneficiaries, Eligible Designated Beneficiaries, or Nondesignated Beneficiaries.

Simply stated, a Designated Beneficiary is a person named on the beneficiary form. An Eligible Designated Beneficiary is a person who is a:

- A spouse;
- Minor child of the account owner;
- Disabled;
- Chronically ill person, or;
- None of the above, but a person not more than 10 years younger than the account owner.

A Nondesignated Beneficiary is a beneficiary who is not a Designated Beneficiary. In other words, a non-person such as a trust.

The classification of a beneficiary is important because the distribution possibilities are different. In some cases, there is a life expectancy option. In other cases, there is a five-year distribution requirement. In other cases, the full 10-year rule is available. This is another example of why you should seek counsel from a professional to determine your most tax-efficient options.

Naming a Trust as The Beneficiary

One note on this point. I continue to be amazed at how uninformed financial advisors are about who to name as the beneficiary of IRAs or other qualified plan accounts.

Too many financial advisors are just not up to date on the advantages and disadvantages of naming your trust as the primary beneficiary of your retirement account. I guess we really shouldn't expect them to be. When I hear clients say that their financial advisor told them they could not name their trust as the primary beneficiary of their IRA, I just shake my head.

Clearly, after the SECURE Act you can still name a trust as the beneficiary of your IRA. If the trust is correctly structured, the trust would be the Designated Beneficiary. To qualify as a Designated Beneficiary and have distributions treated as if they are made to a "person," the trust must meet specific requirements. The trust must be valid under state law. It must become irrevocable upon the IRA owner's death. It must identify beneficiaries of the IRA, and the plan administrator or custodian must receive a copy of the trust on or before October 31st in the year following the IRA owner's death.

If the trust qualifies as a Designated Beneficiary, it can be structured as either a Conduit Trust or Accumulation Trust. In a Conduit Trust, all distributions from the plan administrator will be passed from the administrator to your successor trustee and on to your beneficiary. The trust is merely a flow-through vehicle. By contrast, with an Accumulation Trust, your trustee has the option to withhold distributions to comply with other distribution requirements of the trust. There are tax and other considerations to consider if utilizing an Accumulation Trust. With either the Conduit Trust or Accumulation Trust, the beneficiary form must be carefully crafted to ensure each beneficiary of your trust can use their life expectancy in determining distributions.

Those are the highlights of the SECURE Act. There are many rules to follow and deadlines to follow. From an estate planning point of view, these assets should remain titled in your individual name. You recall our recommendation that all assets be titled in the name of your trust. This is one of the exceptions.

Laws that impact estate, financial, and tax planning are always changing. A review of a few of the most recent conversations in Washington, D.C follows.

Possible Tax Attacks

To keep this material as evergreen as possible, I want to invest a page or two reviewing tax issues. These conversations ebb and flow back and forth and often settle based on which political party is in control of Congress and the White House. So, think of what follows as issues you should monitor.

The tax game reminds me of a game of whack-a-mole. Tax reform is typically a tax increase. It reminds me of situations in which repeated efforts to resolve a problem are frustrated by the problem reappearing in a different form. Trying to get on top of malicious tax reform is like playing whack-a-mole.

Some of the tax increase measures discussed at this time are old news. They are recycled every few years. That said, other tax increase ideas have emerged for the first time. Once they emerge, they seldom disappear. Therefore, a brief review is warranted. In many cases, it feels like a giant taffy pull between competing parties and philosophies.

For example, one political party might want to lower the estate tax exclusion to help raise revenue to offset their spending programs. The other party might want to increase the exclusion because they believe assets in the estate have already been taxed multiple times and that death is not, nor should it be, a taxable event. The estate tax exclusion is always in the discussion as are many of the concepts in this chapter. You should watch conversations around these topics very carefully.

Anytime major spending packages are passed by Congress, there has to be some attempt to keep the legislation "revenue-neutral". The current administration is backing significant spending increases and is committed to raising your taxes. A recent headline in the Wall Street Journal indicated that the current White House resident is pushing for "Wartime Tax Rates".

With the current party controlling all three branches of government, we are seeing efforts to make the most significant overhaul of the United States tax code since 1976 to help pay for their spending policies. As of this writing, Congress passed, and the president signed the infrastructure bill. It did not contain any of the off-setting tax increases. Does that mean we are safe from new tax legislation at a later date? Who knows? We passed the $30 trillion mark in total national debt a few days ago. At some point, that data point will have to be addressed, voluntarily or otherwise.

Now we assume the physician's role and conduct a more thorough examination of various tax proposals that could impact your estate plan. We should carefully observe possible changes. A review of the most significant proposals comes next.

Increasing Income Tax Rates

Although more than 100 million U.S. households, or 61% of all taxpayers, paid no federal income taxes last year, the top 20% of taxpayers paid 78% of federal income taxes in 2020, up from 68% in

2019, and the top 1% of taxpayers paid 28% of taxes in 2020, up from 25% in 2019[8]. Yet, we often hear, the rich must pay their fair share.

Recent proposals would increase the top individual rate from 36% to 39.6% on the individual income tax side. Those seeking revenue always advocate other increases in the top marginal rate through additional measures. For example, phasing out itemized deductions. That lifts the rate by about 1.2 percent and raises the top marginal rate to 40.9 percent.

It is more than surprising when someone runs for president while promising to increase social security taxes and gets elected! The campaign and media focused on how benefits for social security recipients would increase. Little was said about who was going to pay it or how.

Here's how.

Payroll Tax Bombs

Again, a standard mantra. Increase taxes on the wealthy. The current administration calls for the 12.4% Social Security tax to be levied on earned income over $400,000. For those taxpayers, that raises the top overall rate to 53.3. This Social Security tax maneuver was used before when Democrats removed the cap on the Medicare tax. Now add that 3.8% and we have a top rate 57.1%.

That pain would only be felt only by a few taxpayers. Politically, the rest of us did not care or failed to notice. We typically acquiesce to

---

[8] Tax Policy Center, 2020.

a tax increase that does not impact our pocketbook. Perhaps this is the beginning of people being aware that the Medicare and Social Security systems are running out of money and must be replenished if we intend to keep our promises to future retirees who have paid into the system.

In his campaign, Biden said those earning over $400,000 per year would be asked to contribute an additional $750 billion over ten years to help. No one blinked an eye. The problem occurs when the actuaries tell the politicians three-quarters of a trillion dollars is not enough to cover the shortfall. Eventually, we will have to impose the tax on everyone with earned income.

Increasing Corporate Taxes

On the corporate tax side, Biden's plan increases the top rate from 21% to 28% and imposes steep new taxes on multinational income. There is some relief in the form of allowing the continuation of current expensing for capital purchases.

There is constant debate about the fairness of the U.S. corporate tax structure. Should U.S. companies pay U.S. taxes on their revenue, even if it is generated and taxed in a foreign country? Or should we have a "territorial" system like many other countries that require U.S. companies pay tax only on revenue generated in the U.S.? There are always debates about the balance between the rate of tax corporations pay and at what level it makes our companies less competitive.

Somewhere along the line people forgot that corporations do not pay taxes. Their balance sheet may indicate they do, when in reality, taxes they incur are offset by increased productivity, higher prices for their products, reduced dividends, layoffs, tax credits the government provides, or less money to spend for business expansion.

The point is, if you are a business owner and are taxed as a "C" corporation, you should pay attention to this discussion. As with many proposals, politicians always attempt to finagle the new law, so it avoids much attention by taxing only the "wealthy," whatever that means.

Capital Gains Rules Change

This is another often-used proposal to raise revenue. It has some political appeal but ignores the fact that when capital gains taxes are lower, revenue collected by the government from the sale of long-held assets increases. Yet, increasing the capital gains tax rate comes up on a recurring basis. Some believe it will generate enough revenue to provide more funding for social programs.

How does the capital gains tax work? The sale of a capital asset generally triggers capital gains (or losses). The taxable gain is the difference between a capital asset's selling price and the investment's original cost, adjusted upward for improvements and lowered for depreciation deductions. The asset could be farmland, stocks, mutual funds, or investment real estate. In other words, any capital asset that has grown in value since its acquisition.

If Stan and Betsy purchased a stock for $5,000 and sold it for $45,000, they would report a capital gain of $40,000 on their next year's 1040. If the asset is held for more than one year, the tax rate applied to the gain is typically less than the rates you pay on ordinary income items such as wages.

The theory behind a lower capital gains tax rate is that investors should be encouraged to take investment risk to aid business start-ups and job creation. If successful, the investor should be rewarded for their investment and efforts by paying a lower tax rate when selling those assets. That has been U.S. philosophy and policy for nearly a century. It has worked well and spurred capital formation in our economy.

Some administrations like to test that theory and want to boost the capital-gains rate for wealthy individuals from 23.8% to 43.6%, including the 3.8% Medicare tax. That is about an 80% increase in current rates. Some of you may be thinking, "Should I sell everything before that happens?"

Here is some good news for many of us. This proposal to increase the capital gains rates would only apply to income for sales above $1 million. See how politicians manipulate these proposals to avoid political fallout? That said, more of us than imagined will be hit. Will family farms be exempt? The sale of a residence? How about the sale of a closely held business? While the tax rate on capital gains is often on the table, here is an idea that is seldom mentioned. It deserves our careful attention.

Eliminating the Step-Up Rule

This is a dagger. I previously covered this topic a couple of times in the book. This agenda item is one new proposal that will impact most of us. The current revenue enhancement (tax increase) idea is to eliminate the current rules allowing your heirs to receive a stepped-up tax basis on assets they inherit from you. What does "basis step-up" mean, and how does it work?

I covered the concept in detail. Here's another example for reinforcement. Assume you acquired a ten-unit apartment building in 2000 for $500,000. The IRC allows you to recognize depreciation of the building (not the land) as a legitimate expense. Therefore, adding the formulaic depreciation expense to your property's operating statement lowers your annual taxable income. Assume depreciation benefits during your ownership have totaled $150,000. That amount reduces your tax basis to $350,000. Further, assume you made additional investments in the property of $50,000. Improvements are added to your tax basis. Now your tax basis is $400,000. Last month you sold the property for $800,000. Your taxable gain is the sales price less your tax basis, or $800,000 - $400,000 (tax basis) = a $400.000 taxable gain.

We know the current step-up rule allows your heirs to re-set the tax cost of your appreciated assets to the asset's fair market value at the time of your death. The effect is that if your heirs sell those assets for that same fair market value established at your death, they pay no capital gains tax. They would only pay tax on any realized increase in value above the fair market value set at your death.

Applied to our example in the above paragraph, that means if shortly after your passing, your heirs sold the property for $800,000, their tax basis is stepped-up to the fair market value of the asset set at the time of your death. They would pay zero capital gains tax.

Used wisely, the step-up rule can "disappear" capital gains taxes.

Eliminating the step-up rule means your original tax basis stays intact for your heirs. Your tax basis would be their tax basis. When selling the assets, your heirs would use your tax basis when calculating Uncle Sam's share of the proceeds. The result is your heirs pay the same capital gain tax you would have paid if you sold the assets during your lifetime. Now, back to our example, if your heirs sold the property, they would have a taxable gain of $400,000. By the way, this is in addition to paying estate taxes that may be owed.

Historically, the media and political narrative from those with spend-and-tax preferences profess the new tax proposals only apply to the "wealthy." They always discount the law of unintended consequences. I suspect many of the tax increases will eventually apply to middle-class families. There is simply not enough of the "wealthy" to cover the recent proposals, even if you taxed them at a 100% rate. The plan to tax inherited assets on your original tax basis (cost) rather than allowing the basis to be adjusted to fair market value at the time of death will cause a large spike in taxes for the heirs of many of you. This is especially true in the case of inheriting businesses. Many business owners deposited $50 in the bank 20 years ago and started working. Their tax basis is zero or close to it.

Here is another example of a business transaction from a recent Ernst & Young report. I paraphase:

"...someone started a wine distribution company two decades ago. The business initially had no market value. When that founder dies in 2025, his daughter inherits the company, now worth $550,000 with annual revenues of $40,000.

Under current law, the company's value for tax purposes would be "stepped up" to the fair market value at dad's death. His daughter would not owe capital gains taxes on her inheritance. Next, assume she continues to grow the distributorship's value and decides to sell it five years later for $710,000. Under current law, she would owe the 23.8% capital gains tax on its appreciation under her wing, or approximately $38,000 ($710,000-$550,000 = $160,000; $160,000 x .238 = $38,080).

Now assume the step-up rule is abolished. She wouldn't owe tax upon inheriting and running the business her father started — but neither would it get a stepped-up basis. When she eventually sells the company for $710,000, she would owe capital gains tax, at the proposed higher rate, on its total gains since it started from zero. That's a tax bill of more than $281,000 ($710,000 x .396 = $281,160). That means her tax bill is more than seven times higher!"

This is obviously a massive hike and a terrible burden for all but the wealthiest individuals. It is likely to create debt for many, and a resulting fire sale in small businesses. Unless there is a carve-out in the proposal, closely held businesses, farm and ranch operations and your personal residence could be exposed to this tax regime.

Taxation of Retirement Accounts

Retirement accounts have been a target of the spend and tax crowd for some time. It's simple. That's where the money is. The attack could come in a variety of forms. They could modify current laws by limiting or ending the deductibility of IRA and employer-based 401K contributions.

They could limit the use of Roth accounts. Spend and tax politicians do not like the fact that distributions from a retirement account can be tax-free, even if you paid tax on the contributions many years ago and even though the value of your Roth holdings are included in your gross estate for estate tax purposes.

Currently, 100% of distributions from a traditional IRA or 401k are subject to ordinary income taxation. If the politicians raise the personal income tax rate, you will have less money in your pocket from your retirement account distributions.

Wealth Tax

One U.S. Senator – who will remain unnamed but hails from a Northeastern state that is home to the Boston Red Sox and New England Patriots and who claimed a false native about her Native American heritage - wants to impose an annual wealth tax on the fair market value of your assets.

Thus far, this plan has not gained much traction. Yet the narrative lingers. It will not stick at this point but will surely be on the agenda of possibilities when considering future revenue generators.

Significant issues surround the enforcement of a wealth tax, including valuation, adjustments, how the government will reimburse taxpayers when values decline, and the tax effect on assets that must be sold to pay the annual tax, among others. By the way, there would be no reimbursements. The government would simply hold your overpayment and use it to offset any future tax you may owe. Interest-free, of course.

The Estate and Gift Tax Exclusion

We have covered how the current rules apply. A review of the basics is in order. We know you can transfer up to a specific amount of your assets after deducting debt (in other words, your net worth) without incurring an estate tax. If there is an estate tax, it is the responsibility of your estate, not your heirs, to pay the tax.

The estate tax and gift taxes are currently unified. This means you can utilize your exclusion with gifts during your lifetime and transfers at the time of your death. Said another way, lifetime gifts will be charged against your lifetime exclusion.

There is an exception for gifts you make each year. Current law allows you to make gifts every year up to $16,000 to as many individuals as you choose. These annual gift limits are indexed for inflation, meaning the gift amount allowed each year increases over time. Moreover, annual gifts falling below the exclusion amount are not charged against your lifetime gift and estate tax exclusion.

Planning opportunities for annual tax-free gifting are often overlooked and under-utilized by many families. The annual gift exclusion can be especially valuable in the context of life insurance purchases. Structured correctly in tandem with an irrevocable trust, you can ensure that the policy death benefits distributed to your heirs will be both income and estate tax-free. It is a powerful funding source for families who will owe estate taxes or have a need for liquidity at the time of a death.

As of this writing in early 2022, the estate tax exclusion has been adjusted for inflation and now sits at $12.06 million per person. We also know that on January 1, 2026, current law provides that the current exclusion reverts back to $5.49 million, again adjusted for inflation. That should create an exclusion amount of slightly over $6 million. With proper estate tax planning, our example couple, Stan and Betsy, would each be entitled to an exclusion and could transfer up to $24.12 million to anyone of their choosing and pay no federal estate tax.

> **Be careful. Today's large estate tax exclusion disappears on January 1, 2026!**

Current law also provides that if the deceased spouse does not utilize or require the use of their entire exclusion, the unused portion can be "ported" over to the survivor and added to their remaining exclusion. Again, with proper planning, this portability feature assures both spouses' exclusions are fully available to each of them at the time of their death.

Any assets you leave to your surviving spouse are not counted in the total amount subject to estate tax. The right of spouses to leave any amount to one another is known as the unlimited marital deduction. But when the surviving spouse who inherited those assets dies, if the value of all the survivor's assets exceeds the exclusion amount, the beneficiaries may then owe estate taxes. Other deductions, including charitable donations or any debts or fees that come with the estate, are also excluded from the final calculation.

Other than modifying the personal and corporate tax rates and thresholds, the estate tax draws our attention and ignites vigorous political and tax debate. Those debates extend beyond the economic to the social and political.

Opponents of the estate tax assert it is a "death tax," that death is not a taxable event as described in the Internal Revenue Code, and that the tax is a disincentivizing business destruction policy.

Those favoring reduction or elimination of the exclusion argue the current large exclusion is a "silver spoon" policy favoring the wealthy and that 99.8 percent of estates owe no estate tax at all[9]. You decide. Even though few estates are subject to estate tax, repealing the estate tax would be a massive windfall for the federal government.

Proposals have centered on either reducing the current exclusion or increasing the rate once the exclusion threshold is reached. Recent ideas centered on raising the top estate tax rate to 45% from 40% while lowering the exclusion to as low as $3.5 million. Perhaps the politicians promoting the idea should review their personal financial statements first. Lowering the exclusion this much and raising the estate tax rate would dramatically alter the estate tax for the politicians and many families.

More aggressive proposals separate the gift tax from the estate tax and limit the amount of lifetime gifts to $1 million, including any amounts you gift using the annual gift exclusion.

What if a law is passed that lowers the exclusion and eliminates the step-up in tax basis rule? What if Stan and Betsy created a successful small business, owned a farm and ranch operation, or a successful emerging tech company? They might think themselves safe today. Then they discover that they could be paying a combined 68.9% tax on their assets to Uncle Sam based on the capital gain tax and the estate tax.

---

[9] According to the Joint Committee on Taxation.

Do I have your attention yet?

Enforcement of the Internal Revenue Code

The new Senate bi-partisan infrastructure deal is not a done deal yet. Supporters say there will be no tax increase to fund this part of the Biden administration's spending spree. Oh, but wait. Biden's recent $1.75 trillion spending plan includes an $80 billion expansion of the IRS staffing and other expenditures to more aggressively enforce tax revenue collection. The specific goal of this arrangement is to increase the number of IRS audits of taxpayers, especially small businesses, and extract $100 billion in additional tax revenue without raising taxes.

The underlying premise of this measure is that the administration believes millions of people are cheating on their tax returns and that increasing audits will produce an explosion of revenue. We can expect a much heavier hand from the IRS in the upcoming years. This will heighten the importance of asset valuations when pursuing gift and estate tax strategies.

What Does This Mean?

Clearly, no one knows which, if any, of these ideas will make it into law. There is an unlimited amount of creativity on the part of some in our nation's capital when it comes to extracting more money from taxpayers. Those considering fully utilizing the current $12.06 million estate and gift tax exclusion through gifting strategies should consider your options as soon as possible. In the current political environment, delaying these planning strategies becomes much riskier and their validity more uncertain.

The reform list is lengthy. It should be noted that there is legal precedent for the law to claw back gains or gifts made at earlier times to impose higher taxes. The U.S. Treasury Department stated it would not claw back 2021 gifts into your taxable estate at death. We should be skeptical that this will hold. In fact, there are just released proposals about recapturing tax on recent gifting strategies. Utilizing the "Oh, that will never happen" strategy to protect your assets would not be clear thinking.

There is speculation about how many taxpayers there may be who earn less than $400,000 but may have enough capital gains on unsold assets to qualify for the higher rates, and their heirs would have to pay taxes at those same rates upon their death.

It is difficult to predict how this will shake out and what changes will get signed into law. I shared this chapter to review a few basic principles we covered before and alert you to possible tax reform areas. Meanwhile, seek great counsel for your estate and income tax planning. Couple it with an analysis of your investments and consider various options in your planning. Do it now and keep your ear very close to the ground.

We have covered a multitude of points about who needs to implement an estate plan, why it is important, and a few of the crucial components of a plan. We addressed considerations for retirees, business and farm and ranch owners, a few details about the planning with retirement accounts, and threats to the current tax rules that might negatively impact your estate.

There is one other topic I want to address that can impact the success of protecting your estate. Take a look.

The Inheritance Effect

O ne of the biggest dilemmas that affluent families face is the so-called third-generation curse. It states that the majority of families will lose both their wealth and their business by the time it reaches the third generation. There is an old Chinese saying that goes "Wealth does not last beyond three generations". The American version, "Shirtsleeves to shirtsleeves in three generations" expresses the same sentiment. There is data to back up these aphorisms.

This is a tender topic, one too often addressed by whispers, innuendo, deflection, denial, and avoidance. It reminds me of the popular *Mission Impossible* television show from the late 1960s. That show inspired the currently popular movie sequences of the same name starring Tom Cruise.

At the beginning of each show, the show's star, Jim Phelps (portrayed by Peter Graves), would turn on a tape player and listen to a message delivered by an authoritative voice describing what seemed an almost "impossible" mission. The message always ends by clearly stating the mission, then close by saying, "As always, should you or any of your IM Force be caught or killed, the secretary will disavow any knowledge of your actions. This tape will self-destruct in five seconds. Good luck, Jim."

Jim Phelps and his skilled team understood the mission, overcame the challenges, and carried it out. Successfully. Too often, when successful families transfer wealth to the younger generation, the mission fails. There is no Jim Phelps to clarify the mission and help execute it.

Nearly everyone in the family knows the mission. Parents know what needs to be done and what needs to be said. Too often, what's missing is the coaching is required to ensure the next generation of those who inherit wealth understand how it is created, the price that was paid, how it grows, and the parent's expectations for handling and protecting it. This mission should start far in front of creating an estate plan.

Without this guidance, a danger zone is created. What some refer to as the *Inheritance Effect* can take root. An example is useful.

Stan has enjoyed a successful career. Betsy is an entrepreneur and shrewd marketer who built a successful business worth $20 million. Both of their children, Susan and John, are great young people. Susan works in the business where she applies her CPA credentials and accounting skills. John does little and benefits from the fact that Stan and Betsy do not want him to experience the hardships they experienced. They want, and the children want, the lifestyle they experienced growing up. Very little was ever asked of the kids and John took them up on it. His response to those circumstances can best be described as lethargic. After getting his graduate business degree, he decided all the offers were way below his capability. In his early 30s, John has never held a job. He gets all the money he needs from Stan and Betsy.

With the benefit of hindsight, the seeds of an entitlement mentality were planted early. Always told how smart they were, neither child was praised for how hard they worked or the effort they were making to achieve something meaningful. After a setback, all John and Susan heard was, "…don't worry, it doesn't matter." Or, "you shouldn't have to do that." When John was offered entry-level positions commensurate with his education and experience, all he could hear was his parents saying, "…you deserve better."

When each of them reached 16, they were given a new car. One of them totaled their car within weeks, only to receive a new model. John began to believe rules did not apply to him. With no expectations set and no accountability in place, he believed that he would always be taken care of. The word "responsibility" was nowhere to be found in the unopened dictionary lying on his desk.

There is no need to go further. You get the point. John became infected with the *Inheritance Effect*. Unless it is addressed early, it is difficult to overcome later in life.

That was one of the great things about being raised in a small town and farm environment when I was young. There are always chores to be done on a farm. Always. When you were tasked with a job, it was given as a responsibility and accepted as a commitment. If your job was to build a new fence or upgrade a quarter-mile of a faulty fence needing repair, you better do it right, or a dozen heifers might escape. If lost, or if they died, that was a serious financial setback to the farm operation.

Some of us make things too easy for our children. We fear they are not strong enough to survive life's bumps and bruises. We place far too much emphasis on the words "success" and "failure". There is no such thing. Those words carry far more emotional baggage than they deserve. There are only outcomes. It's better to think in terms of outcomes and results. We either get the results we want or we do not. Simple as that. We innovate, adapt, and continue forward if desired results do not occur.

What does this have to do with estate planning? Everything. If it is appropriate and if you care about what happens to your hard-earned wealth, regardless of size, you have a responsibility to educate your children about money. Or, see to it they are mentored by someone who can educate them about money and its attendant responsibility. It goes far beyond showing them how to do their job at work. "I gave them every opportunity", or "I did the best I could", is not enough. If you don't know how to coach and mentor your child about your success, your wealth, and how you expect them to handle it, find and collaborate with someone who has the experience to help.

The price of the *Inheritance Effect* can be very high. I have seen uncoached children who have inherited money start believing it was not their money (of course not), then think they do not deserve it, and finally develop a mental illness around the topic of money. I have seen inheritors believe that because the money was not theirs, they could give it all away, often to the chagrin of other family members and employees who are dedicating a lifetime to helping parents create a great company. I have seen a son or daughter-in-law ruin relationships due to their misunderstanding of how to use and prudently manage the wealth created by their spouse's family. And, I have seen spendthrift children of frugal parents think the money will never run out. It is tragic when it does.

The *Inheritance Effect* is real. It is an invisible, dangerous mindset that attaches early, grows with time, leaves permanent scars and deleterious consequences. When you are creating your estate plan, it is a perfect time to have these discussions with a professional who has very likely witnessed this with other clients. There is no one size fits all approach to addressing the *Inheritance Effect*. It would be wise to add this to the list of considerations when selecting an estate planning attorney. Look for one who identifies as an Attorney & Counselor at Law rather than merely an Attorney at Law. A significant amount of counseling occurs in a successful estate planning process.

Though we have witnessed "Shirtsleeves to shirtsleeves in three generations" up close and personal, it does not have to be that way. Valuable tools and approaches provide guidance to influence behaviors that protect generational wealth and preserve estates.

For now, we modify the *Mission Impossible* narrative to make the point. "Mr. Phelps, your mission is to successfully educate your children about the *Inheritance Effect*. We are providing the tools that will help achieve the mission. As always, should you or any of your family fail to achieve this mission, the secretary will disavow any knowledge of your actions, and your family will suffer the consequences. This tape will self-destruct in five seconds. Good luck, Jim."

Getting Started

By now you may be thinking, "Okay, I get it. It's time to get this part of my life in order". If so, you will find what comes next useful. If you do not think it is time, re-read the Preface.

The Critical First Step

Since you are at this point in the book you may have read it in its entirety. You now have a good overview of some of the many dimensions of estate planning. Now, what will you do with your new and more complete understanding? Will your family thank you? Only if action follows your new understanding.

The most important "next step" is to find an attorney to help you navigate the estate planning process. Not just any attorney.

You want to find an experienced attorney to help you assess your current situation – your "As Is" and clarify your goals.

You want to find an experienced attorney who will ask questions you may not have considered. Some of those questions and conversations around them may be uncomfortable.

You want to find an experienced attorney who will guide you to a plan design that will achieve your estate planning objectives.

You will want to find an experienced attorney who can outline the benchmarks and timelines for successfully implementing your plan.

Remember, effective and appropriate estate planning is not about how much money you have. It is about what you want to happen at different stages in your life. An estate planning attorney with deep experience and expertise will help.

An experienced professional will outline various scenarios and ask questions that make you dig. They will have you play the lead role in multiple scenarios so you can experience the implications for yourself and your family. When you clarify how that scenario would apply to your situation, they will join you in exploring how to best address it.

That is what people pay for when they work with our firm. I tell people our legal documents are free. There is no charge for the paper. You pay for our experience, our skill at helping you discover what is most important to you, what possible events can occur, and then identify the best solutions given your family situation and your estate planning goals.

Finding an attorney to facilitate the design of your plan is about finding an estate planning partner. It is essential to implement an effective estate plan successfully. There are so many scenarios that people are not aware of or fail to consider. Failure to address them could put your goals – even your financial future - at risk.

Look for an attorney with in-depth experience, a professional whose experience is deep, not wide. Not broad, like some practitioners. Deep. The attorney in my hometown in Northwest Missouri knows more about a wider variety of legal topics than I ever will. The wide variety of demands of that small community with two attorneys requires him to have a broad-based practice. For estate planning, you are better off with a specialist.

> **Find an estate planning attorney who is committed to this area, not just curious about it.**

As an example, our firm focuses exclusively on estate and elder law planning and business succession or sales transactions. Our depth of knowledge and expertise in those areas reflect the seriousness of our commitment to these topics. Find a specialized estate planning attorney rather than someone practicing across multiple areas, an attorney committed to the practice area, not just curious about it.

Addressing the topic of who you should hire leads back to the initial confusion that holds people back from taking steps to get a plan set up. If you call any law firm and say, "Hey, I need help with an estate plan, can you help?" The answer is always going to be "Yes."

You have to go beyond that. Examine what the attorneys have done in their past, how many estate plans they have created. Probe to discover what they have learned from their experience, what steps they have taken to become an authority in the field, and what credibility they have.

Find somebody you feel you can partner with, then explore how they handle the planning process for clients. A partner is a careful listener. A partner knows how to ask questions, and a partner knows how to lead a conversation about delicate topics and family matters.

You want this to be a life-long relationship, not a transaction.

Further Thoughts on Finding an Estate Planning Attorney

We are members of the American Academy of Estate Planning Attorneys. You would be well-served to work with a member of the Academy. Membership in the Academy is an indicator of a firm's commitment to the field. It is also an indicator of their expertise. Academy members have in-depth knowledge and serious expertise in this field.

Find someone who will complete your work for a fixed investment, not an hourly billing rate. With hourly billing, the entire risk of the cost is on you. You have little control over what the attorney decides to charge. If your attorney utilizes a fixed investment to complete your plan, they absorb most of the investment risk. If they are good, they will scope the work much more carefully than you might experience with hourly billing. They have a business to run. If they misjudge the type, nature, and extent of the service required, your work might not be profitable.

A note about the previous point. You want your work to be profitable for your attorney. Why? Because we have seen many attorneys try to low-ball fixed fees to complete an estate plan. Guess what? When you need them the most, they are no longer in business. You want them there for you when you and your family need them the very most.

Finally, find someone who will give you some assurances about the timeline for the completion of your work. Once you decide to design a plan and create a plan, you do not want this to take six months. I learned that obvious lesson from my experience with my father. Fate intervenes.

As a reminder from a previous statement, the documents are free. You pay for our experience, our depth of knowledge, and the steps we take to ensure that your plan is perfect the day it is completed. These are the elements of a relationship, not a transaction.

As part of the process, you will share information about your assets. This will include you having to share information about what may be confidential. Remember, this is an attorney-client relationship. Information you share with your attorney will be confidential.

You can have a great experience with setting up your estate plan. When completed, you will have a sense of accomplishment, an awareness that you did a wonderful thing for your family. You will sense a previously unknown peace of mind.

Many of us, like my father, create a list of resolutions at the beginning of each year. Perhaps like his 3x5 index card, your resolutions say something similar to, "Other: Complete Trust". The problem is life gets in the way. The same items appear on the list year after year after year. Once your estate plan is completed, it will be a welcome sense of relief and a great satisfaction.

Be a Hero to Your Family

With our overview of the estate planning process, we have outlined any number of risks you and your family are exposed to when there is no plan in place. Everyone in your family is vulnerable to uncertainty and unanticipated problems.

We have also identified a variety of estate planning issues and possible ways to address them in a meaningful way. You now know estate planning is all about protecting you and your assets. You now know better ways to protect yourself during your lifetime. You now know why we prefer a revocable trust as the foundation of your plan. You now know better ways to ensure the transfer of your hard-earned money is as seamless as possible by avoiding probate and having appropriate decision-makers in charge of settling your estate. You now have a feel for the possible changes to tax laws that might negatively impact your estate.

If you are still wondering if you need a plan, or what kind of plan you need, do this for me. Take a blank sheet of paper and draw a large "T" with the horizontal line a couple of inches from the top of the page and the vertical line beginning in the middle of the horizontal line and extending straight down to the bottom. On the left side, list the "Pros" of completing your plan. On the other side, list the "Cons".

Make your list. Notice most of the items listed on the Con side are focused on you. Too complicated. Too expensive. Takes too long. There are hard decisions to make. Don't know which attorney to choose.

On the other hand, all the reasons why it makes good sense to create an estate plan. Do you wish to have some protection if you become incapacitated? Do you worry about taxes or exposing your estate to probate? Do you want to be a burden to your children? Are you prepared to pay for your nursing home costs? Are you going to take the position that you will just let the kids figure it out? What does that say about the love relationship in the family? Is that the act of a responsible person? Go ahead, and think about what you currently know and what you learned from this book. Complete your list.

Which side weighs heavier?

Still struggling? As many we work with have told us, either they do not have an estate plan in place or have a plan that is inadequate for their current situation. They tell us they know they are vulnerable, at least to some extent. They tell us they know their family is not protected as well as they could be. They tell us they don't want to be a burden to their children.

There is an old story about George S. Hellman, a book dealer, who once offered financier J.P. Morgan the famous Wakefield collection of manuscripts of great American authors. One of the manuscripts contained this short poem:

Between the dark and the daylight
When the night is beginning to lower
Comes a pause in the day's occupations
That is known as the children's hour.

Your decision to create a plan communicates a powerful love message to your family. Is it your children's hour? They will react to your decision. I promise.

Stop for a minute and picture this. Your family is sitting around the kitchen table. You may be incapacitated, or you have passed away. Sadness and anxiety fill the room. The look on each child's face is disbelief. Then a few days pass. Another family conversation ensues. Now comes the business of trying to figure out the next steps.

What must be done to either protect the estate during your incapacity or distribute your estate if you have passed away? A family member asks, what kind of planning did mom and dad have? Who's in charge? The search begins. Phone calls are made to no avail. There doesn't seem to be a plan, except perhaps a last will dated in 1984. What does that mean? Someone suggests contacting an attorney. There is a scavenger hunt to determine your assets and accounts. When found, asset ownership is reviewed. It's all over the place. More time passes. Hope gives way to disappointment. Frustration sets in when the implications of not having a plan sink in.

Listen carefully as you hear your children say, "I can't believe mom and dad left us this mess. This is going to be a heavy lift and cost us a small fortune. Who has time to do this? How did this happen? Why?"

Can you see them? Hear the words?

There is another possibility. You create an estate plan. You keep it up to date. When you make the plan, you clearly state your expectations to all concerned. Now hear the voices. Your family is saying, "We are so proud of mom and dad for doing this for us. They are so responsible. It's so like them to prepare us for this."

Can you see that picture? Hear the conversation?

There will be a conversation, and a picture will emerge. None of the "reasons why" we fail to plan will refute the feelings expressed at that table.

Which picture do you want you and your family to be in?

Take this first step. Explore your options. Get a plan put in place. Do it now. You will be communicating a message of responsibility and love for your family. You will be setting an example of doing the right thing. You will create a peace of mind for yourself and a sense of satisfaction that will empower and help protect you throughout your lifetime.

In closing, thank you for sharing your time with me on this important topic. Godspeed in your journey to creating terrific life and a terrific estate plan.

About Parman & Easterday PLLC

Thank you for your interest in estate planning. This book covers only a few basics and is certainly not a comprehensive guide to the process of creating your estate plan.

To learn more about your specific needs regarding estate planning, elder law issues, business succession planning for family businesses or selling your business to a third-party, we invite you to request our free reports, webinars, and DVDs. They will add to your knowledge base and clarify your thinking.

If you have any questions about your business, tax/financial or estate strategies in this new environment, go to www.parmanlaw.com or call our office at 405-843-6100 to arrange an appointment.

We are proud of our Purpose, Vision, Mission, and Core Values statements.

- Our Purpose - We exist to empower you to design your future and live your dreams.
- Our Vision - A world in which people experience joy, abundance, and freedom.
- Our Mission - To create unique strategies and solutions that preserve and protect our clients' personal and financial futures.
- Our Core Values – we are dependable, we keep commitments, we expand our level of competence, we have a team and client-first attitude, and we do the right thing.

Our entire business model is set up to educate people about estate planning and how best to create the perfect plan for them at that time. Our books, blogs, online and Pony Express newsletters, articles and Special Reports, client education events, and Legacy Care program serve as a forum where clients can learn more about estate and financial planning in a non-threatening environment. They also exemplify our commitment to strengthening our expertise and our dedication to helping our clients get this right for themselves and their families.

We are also proud of our American Academy of Estate Planning Attorneys membership. The Academy requires us to seek constant improvement in our expertise and how we serve our clients. Complying with their rigorous membership requirements is one example of our commitment to the field of estate planning, to getting better every day, and always acting in the best interest of our clients. If you are from a state other than Missouri, Kansas, Texas, or Oklahoma, you can visit the Academy website at www.aaepa.com to find the name of an Academy attorney near you.

Acknowledgments

So many people were part of writing this book. It started as a project we thought I could dictate and complete in 60 days. That did not happen.

First, I would like to thank the Parman & Easterday team. Our excellent staff indulged me with the time required for this project. Attorneys Jeff Easterday, Jerry Shiles, Jeff Green, and Tracy Brock contributed their questions, corrections, and suggestions to help make the book more accurate and useful.

Next, I must acknowledge our wonderful clients. We are inspired by your commitment to your families, loyalty to our firm, and continued efforts to help us every day. Your referrals and suggestions about how we can improve our practice add tremendous value to us every day. To all of you, I am eternally grateful.

Darlene Parman, Scott Parman, and Lynn Mills discovered my errors in expression and writing more thoroughly than Sherlock Holmes solved unsolvable crimes. Their input was creative and invaluable. Any remaining flaws in the text remain my doing. Darlene, Scott, and Lynn simply threw their hands up.

Lance Pincock facilitated the publishing of the book. His careful review and suggestions are much appreciated.

I also want to acknowledge Robert Armstrong, Sandy Fisch, Jennifer Price, and the American Academy of Estate Planning Attorneys team. The Academy has been an essential part of our firm since 1993, and I must acknowledge their long-standing contribution to our success.

A Special Free Offer From
Larry V. Parman

For readers of *The Straight Shooter's Guide To Estate Planning*

Dear Reader,

Is this the end or a beginning? If you found value within these pages, I can help you do more than understand what your estate plan should include. If you are from Oklahoma, Missouri, Kansas, or Texas, <u>I can help you beyond the pages of this book. I am offering to buy 30 minutes of my law firm's time - and give it to you. If you reside elsewhere, we will direct you to a fellow American Academy of Estate Planning Attorneys member. They will also serve you well.</u>

What you have read about here is the tip of the estate planning iceberg, merely a few pieces of the puzzle. Getting your estate plan in place is an endeavor most people put off until it is too late. I want to help you avoid that. You are now equipped with the information you need to begin and eventually make the right choices for yourself and your family. Let me help you take the next step and get you legally squared away so that you can rest easy at night knowing that you and your family are protected, regardless of the future.

I'm willing to buy 30 minutes of my time and give it to you for FREE just for reading this book. **Reserve your "Straight Shooter's Get It**

Done Call" and let me and our expert estate planning attorneys answer any questions you have from reading this book. We will also help you clarify the next steps you need to take to get your estate plan completed the right way so you can relax and cross it off your to-do list.

Claim your FREE 30-minute **"Straight Shooter's Get It Done Call"** by calling 405-843-6100 TODAY. Let us know you are a Straight Shooter calling for your FREE 30-minute phone Discovery Consultation.

We look forward to being of service!

About Larry V. Parman

About Larry V. Parman: Author, Attorney at Law & Financial Advisor

His father's untimely death in a farm accident forced Larry and his family into dealing with a lengthy probate and the IRS over the valuation of a farm and small business. At that point, Larry decided his calling was to help families create effective estate plans designed to reduce taxes; minimize legal interference with the transfer of assets to one's loved ones, and protect their assets from predators and creditors.

Since founding Parman & Easterday PLLC in 1985, Larry Parman and his team have used their retirement and investment planning experience to help thousands of families create estate and financial plans.

Larry was a founding member of the American Academy of Estate Planning Attorneys in 1993. Numerous publications and experts such as The *Wall Street Journal, Newsweek, U.S. News & World Report, Money Magazine, Consumer Reports, Money Magazine,* and bestselling financial author Suze Orman recommend using firms that are members of the American Academy of Estate Planning Attorneys for their estate planning needs. As a registered investment advisor, Larry's investment strategies follow the scientific principles of Nobel Prize-winning economists Eugene Fama, Kenneth French, Harry Markowitz, William Sharpe and Merton Miller.

Mr. Parman has co-authored two books on estate planning, *Estate Planning Basics: A Crash Course in Safeguarding Your Legacy* and *Guiding Those Left Behind in Oklahoma: Settling the Affairs of Your Loved One*, with nationally-acclaimed estate planning experts Robert Armstrong and Sanford Fisch, co-founders of the American Academy of Estate Planning Attorneys. Based on his experience as a Registered Investment Advisor, Sydney LeBlanc and Lyn Fisher, nationally-recognized authors, publishers and experts in the financial services industry, asked Parman to be a contributing author for *Stop & Think: Important Financial Advice for You and Your Family,* a book on retirement planning.

Drawing on his business experience, Mr. Parman authored *Above the Fray: Leading Yourself, Your Business and Others During Turbulent Times.* His most recent book, *The Straight Shooter's Guide to Estate Planning* was published in June, 2022.

Larry is also the former host of the radio show *Your Estate Matters* on KTOK and was selected by Prosperity Productions as a featured speaker in a nationally-recognized education show on Living Trusts.

Recognized for his expertise in business development, Mr. Parman served as the State of Oklahoma's Secretary of State and Secretary of Commerce. For the past five years, he has served as the Chairman of the Board of Trustees of the *Oklahoma Council of Public Affairs*, an Oklahoma, a research based think tank focused on policies that encourage free markets, limited government, individual freedom, and the importance of family values and other bulwarks of a civil society.

Notes

Made in the USA
Middletown, DE
02 September 2024

60271608R00157